Nightmare on Main Street

Nightmare on Main Street

Angels, Sadomasochism, and the Culture of Gothic

Mark Edmundson

HARVARD UNIVERSITY PRESS

Cambridge, Massachusetts
London, England

First Harvard University Press paperback edition, 1999

Library of Congress Cataloging-in-Publication Data

Edmundson, Mark, 1952–
Nightmare on Main Street : angels, sadomasochism,
and the culture of Gothic / Mark Edmundson.
p.   cm.
Includes bibliographical references (p.   ) and index.
ISBN 0-674-87484-6 (cloth)
ISBN 0-674-62463-7 (pbk.)
1. Horror tales, American—History and criticism.
2. Gothic revival (Literature)—United States—History—20th century.
3. Popular culture—United States—History—20th century.
4. Horror films—United States—History and criticism.
5. Sadomasochism in literature.   6. Angels in literature.   I. Title.
PS374.G68E36   1997
813´.0872909—dc21   97-20270

FOR LİZ

CONTENTS

PREFACE

Several years ago, for no reason I readily discerned, I began watching horror movies. In the space of twelve months, I must have seen a hundred of them, films like *Night of the Living Dead, Dawn of the Dead, Nightmare on Elm Street, Last House on the Left, Psycho, The People under the Stairs, Texas Chainsaw Massacre.* I talked about horror with some notably strange people inside video stores and out. I flew through obscure books and journals on the subject. In the beginning, I wasn't looking to understand these movies or my need to see them, though as a professor and writer with a penchant for analyzing all significant passing phenomena—and some of the not-so-significant as well—that was probably the logical thing to do. Rather, I wanted new titles, more films to see. I wanted the best, the most frightening and radically conceived movies that the genre offered.

After a while, my ardor waning a little, I became more reflective. A penchant for horror films didn't fit in particularly well with my self-conception. I think of myself as an upbeat type, not entirely unworldly, but still optimistic; someone who, against volumes of current testimony, finds teaching English in a university a fully engaging and a humanly useful thing to do; who has no qualms about bringing children into the world; whose often harsh views on America come out of a wounded but still somehow thriving love for the place. I teach the visionary poets, after all, Shelley, Blake, Emerson, Whitman, writers confident that humanity, or at least some consequential part of it, is capable of dramatic, saving transformation. So what was I doing teaching Shelley's rhapsodic "Ode to the West Wind" by day, then at night repairing to the VCR to watch *Texas Chainsaw Massacre II?* Horror films were for misanthropes, for people who lived in the cellars of their own minds and never wanted to come out. Horror flicks were for losers.

But, I answered myself, saying as much entailed a simple-minded view of these movies. For even in fairly detached terms, some of what I was watching was very good. It's hard to imagine a better directed or more brazenly innovative movie than *Psycho.* (Hitchcock's willingness to kill off his protagonist midfilm, then seduce you into identifying with psycho killer Norman Bates, remains, nearly forty years after the film's release, shocking enough.) Wes Craven's *Nightmare on Elm Street* does a splendid job of dramatizing the oppressive hatred, especially for the young, that can abide behind sanitized institutional appearances. In George Romero's *Dawn of the Dead* one finds a jaggedly violent but well-aimed attack on American consumption and conformity (though maybe the scene where the bikers roar through the shopping mall decapitating the shambling, barely animated zombies—"attention Kmart shoppers"—*is* a bit heavy-handed).

But whatever the caliber of the fare, my horror film watching had an obsessive quality about it. I was getting some kind of cumulative hit from these movies that I wasn't eager to question too closely. For it's possible to use horror films and novels not as a means of insight, but as a way to generate a reductive, bitter version of experience overall. The temptation to take horror's antipathy for virtually all human institutions to the ultimate degree—to see them as intrinsically repressive; calmly crazy, even lethal, in their ministrations—was one to which I could see myself succumbing. So what exactly was I getting into here?

The films I was watching were in what I knew to be the Gothic tradition. As a literary form Gothic was initiated by Horace Walpole in his 1764 novel, *The Castle of Otranto*, then elaborated and intensified by such writers as Monk Lewis, Ann Radcliffe, Mary Shelley and, in America, by Edgar Allan Poe. *Otranto*, which it's said Walpole composed in a furious night of writing, is a tale that features a haunted castle, a mad prince, and frightened heroines in flight, along with a lethal giant helmet; it's a most peculiar book. But it originates the central Gothic conventions, the conventions I was encountering in my horror films: hero-villain, heroine on the run, a terrible place, uncut fear. Much read, *Otranto* was little imitated until the 1790s when, incited by images from the Revolution in France, English writers poured forth Gothic novels. Suddenly all of the passions that the age of reason had banished came back on the wings of the Revolution and in the books of middle-class authors who sometimes frightened themselves with their creations nearly as much as they did their readers.

Gothic, one might say, is the art of haunting, the art of possession. The Gothic artist tries to grab hold of the reader, make it so he can't put the book down, can't think of anything else. In a Gothic fragment, John Keats describes his "living hand," which "would, if it were cold / And in the icy silence of the tomb, / So haunt thy days and chill thy dreaming nights / That thou wouldst wish thine own heart dry of blood / So in my veins red life might stream again."[1] Gothic, at its most aesthetically potent, acts as would Keats's dead, grasping hand; it fills its audience with fear, with an uncanny sense of impending harm, that abides even after the film is over, the book finished and back on the shelf. "See," Keats says, flourishing the hand, "here it is— / I hold it towards you."

Over time I saw that I wasn't the only one in 1990s America who was absorbed by the Gothic. For in our fin de siècle, Gothic novels and films are proliferating. Stephen King and Anne Rice are the dual monarchs, Hades and Persephone, of American Gothic fiction. Their tales of vampires, demons, and ghastly possession probably reach more people than the work of any other American writers. The influence of Alfred Hitchcock, major Gothic artist that he is, remains omnipresent in American film. Quentin Tarantino, David Lynch, the Coen brothers, and Brian de Palma, to name just a few, are Hitchcock's lineal descendants, but there is hardly a suspense or horror picture made in America that doesn't owe a debt to the Master. The kitchen knife that young Michael Myers wields in the opening scene of *Halloween* comes courtesy of Norman and Mrs. Bates.

But what I saw, as I continued to think about my own Gothic fixations and started rereading Poe and Mary Shelley, was that our major Gothic modes are not all fictive. Rather (as my first chapter will show), Gothic conventions have slipped over into ostensibly nonfictional realms. Gothic is alive not just in Stephen King's novels and Quentin Tarantino's films, but in media renderings of the O. J. Simpson case, in our political discourse, in our modes of therapy, on TV news, on talk shows like *Oprah,* in our discussions of AIDS and of the environment. American culture at large has become suffused with Gothic assumptions, with Gothic characters and plots.

There was, it turned out, nothing unusual about my fixation with horror films; in '90s America it seemed that almost everyone was tied up, in one way or another, with the Gothic. If they weren't into slasher movies, it was the *X-Files*, or the Simpson case, serial killers, Rice's vampires, recovered memory, or any of two dozen other extravagances. Gothic isn't everywhere exactly, though once you understand its conventions, Gothic's strong presence is hard to miss.

But that provokes a difficult question. What cultural work is contemporary Gothic doing for its consumers? Why do we need it? Early Gothic writers like Lewis and Radcliffe offered means of insight. They acquainted willing readers with their suppressed passions and allowed them to reflect, however indirectly, on the place of priests and nobles in a revolutionary age. Even in our own time, artists have used Gothic to rouse readers and help them see the world in revealingly darkened shades.

But what about our current, true-life Gothic forms? Do they have any such vitalizing effect? Do Gothic renderings of the Simpson case help us to break through the crust of convention and see race and violence in fresh, if shocking, terms? Does the recovered memory movement, in which young people, mainly women, affirm that they have recaptured memories of abuse, chiefly by parents, lead us to a deeper understanding of gender relations, of sex, of the workings of the unconscious? In other words, to what degree are we as a culture using horror for fresh insight, to what degree to generate sourly reductive versions of experience? (With my horror films, you'll recall, I was doing a little of both.) In the first chapter I try to answer these questions, reflecting on the value of our current culture of Gothic.

In its initial wave, Gothic was the literature of revolution, specifically the revolution in France that dominated European consciousness in the last decade of the eighteenth century. In order to answer questions about Gothic's current workings, I will need to pose large questions about its relations to our own cultural and historical moment. Why Gothic *now?* My answers will be broad ranging, entailing thoughts about religious faith, about the oncoming millennium, and—odd as it may initially sound—about the still potent pressures of the American 1960s on current culture.

One of the major repositories for '90s Gothic is the afternoon talk show. Onto Oprah's stage troop numberless unfortunates, victims and villains. The victims have been pursued, harassed, mistreated. They are sublimely innocent (as any reader of Gothic novels knows they would have to be). The villains present a more interesting case. At first they come across to us as evil incarnate, or simply as monstrous creatures who have gone beyond evil and good. But eventually we learn that they themselves have been victims. They too are haunted by some form of past abuse, so that their bad behavior takes on an air of inevitability. At times, Oprah is an apostle of fate worthy of Edgar Allan Poe: if you were molested by your father, you'll be a molester in turn. There's no way out.

But Oprah speaks in two voices. For at other times, she's a prophet of the will. "I was a welfare daughter just like you . . . how did you let yourself become welfare mothers? Why did you choose this? I didn't."[2] In her second, pseudo-Emersonian guise, Oprah teaches that all is possible, simply through exertions of vital force. It's not hard; just repeat after me.

Oprah's guests are frequently addicted—our current word for the traditional Gothic term "haunted." They're addicted to drugs, sex, shopping, abuse, whatever, and it sometimes seems that there is no hope for them. But periodically Oprah breaks through her nearly Calvinist commitment to predestination and fate. She up and affirms freedom in the most facile terms: you are what you will yourself to be.

From productions like *Oprah* I came to see that interwoven with the '90s culture of Gothic is a culture that seems to be its complete inverse. I call it the culture of facile transcendence. My second chapter, "The World according to Forrest Gump," describes an anti-Gothic world inspired by the belief that self-transformation is as simple as a fairy-tale wish. I focus on the inner-child movement, where you're encouraged to deliver your inner infant from fear and loneliness, on the men's movement, on New Age panaceas, on the mild high that certain kinds of TV can bring, on the angel craze, on power ads, and on other formulas for easy self-remaking that now flourish in the American marketplace. As a culture we've become nearly as obsessed by angels, and guardian angels in particular, as by Gothic images of the serial killer. It's possible, too, to point to a reciprocal relation between our current forms of the Gothic and of facile transcendence: one often creates the need for the other.

Does the proliferation of these forms of facile transcendence substantially challenge the strength of premillennial American Gothic? Is there a creditable yearning for some better form of life, something more affirmative than Gothic pessimism, submerged in these pop modes? I think that sometimes there is, though I find that cultural hope in some of the least likely places, in the kind of popular culture that's most frequently maligned by academic critics and by sophisticated journalists. I also look for alternatives to the culture of Gothic in the past. The second chapter considers the Rousseauianism of the 1960s counterculture, and high modernism as exemplified by the theoretical (not the poetic) T. S. Eliot, as well as by the architects of the modernist school.

But even after identifying a culture of easy transcendence and seeing it in relation to more pervasive Gothic anxieties, I was still left with a riddle. Besides the fact that I had a taste for hyperbole indulged by both forms, I wondered why I would be locked into both Gothic *and* visionary work. How could I be drawn to visionary renewal in the mode of Blake and Emerson and to Gothic horror films? Were the visionary poets in fact what many academic critics now suggest they are: dispensers of a culturally canonized means of facile transcendence? I was still left with what appeared to be an unresolved double life, not unrelated, I couldn't help seeing, to that of the standard Gothic hero-villain. During the day I was teaching Shelley, at night turning on the VCR to imbibe high horror films.

But it gradually came clear to me that the visionary poets were themselves no less interested in the Gothic than I was, though their interest was often of a deeper and more productive sort. It struck me that Blake and Shelley probably found in the horror writers of their day images for those forces, internal and external, that resisted their self-transforming drives. Gothic was a source for Shelley's cruel sky-king Jupiter, and for his mad Count Cenci, just as it was for Blake's inhibiting Spectres and his Selfhood. In part through reading Gothic writers, I imagine, visionaries like Blake and Shelley came up with ways to render their own attractions to absolutism and misogyny. And also to sadomasochism, which I think I can show is the ultimate expression of the Gothic spirit.

In the last chapter, "S & M Culture," I turn to Shelley and Nietzsche, who successfully bring the Gothic and the visionary impulses together in contention and give us images of renewal. Shelley saw his own attraction to sadomasochism and made it the subject of his greatest poem, *Prometheus Unbound*. So Nietzsche, learning I suspect from Shelley, put the Gothic problem of revenge at the core of his thought and worked to find ways to overcome it. America's major visionary, Ralph Waldo Emerson, is himself a Gothic writer—though he is much more than a Gothic writer, too.

But our own Gothic dilemmas are in certain ways different from those faced by Shelley, Nietzsche, and Emerson. Our difficulties centrally involve the attractions of wielding and submitting to absolute power, the attractions of sadomasochism, yes. But our current Gothic crises also erupt from our manifold anxieties about race. Is it possible that the visionary mode might be reinvented for our day, for our particular Gothic traumas? I try to answer that question by looking into two remarkable Gothic works of the American fin de siècle, Toni Morrison's *Beloved* and Tony Kushner's *Angels in America*. My objective, finally, is to do what criticism in its traditional guise often did, to point toward possibilities for future imaginative work.

Rather than seeing ours as a culture of chaos, as many now do, I see it as shot through with a significant dialectical pattern, the play of Gothic and facile transcendence. Naturally there are many important cultural forces that have little to do with either of these phenomena. But to me, reflecting on Gothic and on easy transcendence goes a long way toward helping us make sense of our current circumstances and letting us see how we might better them.

This book is intended as a piece of public criticism. It is not written chiefly for specialists in the Gothic or the so-called Romantic, or for practitioners of what has come to be called cultural studies. *Nightmare on Main Street* ought to be accessible to anyone with an interest in current culture and a willingness to hear it construed from a new angle. It is a speculative book, an attempt at broad cultural diagnosis, thus an essay in the etymological sense. I do not seek comprehensiveness about current culture: many instances of contemporary Gothic and of facile transcendence are not included, or mentioned only in passing. Nor do I strive for a historically inclusive vision of the Gothic: the book shuttles between the late eighteenth and the late twentieth centuries with only a few stopping points between. *Nightmare on Main Street* offers a condensed vision of how things stand with America as the millennium nears, a vision that I hope readers will be able to use in their own attempts to conceive the present and shape the time to come.

I had valuable assistance in developing this book, and it is a pleasure to be able to acknowledge it here. My wife, Elizabeth Denton, read the book at every stage, helping me in numberless ways. Michael Pollan read at least two drafts of the manuscript, and offered fine editorial advice, as well as friendship and encouragement. Richard Rorty made extremely useful suggestions for shaping the argument. Chip Tucker brought his considerable acumen to bear, corrected mistakes, and asked telling questions. Jean Bethke Elshtain responded with remarkable generosity and intelligence. Stephen Smith and Adam Goodheart at *Civilization* reacted warmly to the project, printing a selection from the first chapter in the magazine.

My agent Chris Calhoun, from Sterling Lord, was exemplary in every way; he was an invaluable ally throughout the process. Lindsay Waters, my editor at Harvard, contributed an array of intriguing ideas. For thoughtful editing, thanks to Donna Bouvier. For help on research, I am grateful to Mike Johnson, and also to Tom Roche, Emily DeMarco, and Chris Ruotolo. Thanks to Cynthia Cameros for work on the index and to Virginia Germino for proofreading and more.

American Gothic

Cultural historians of the future, looking to mark the moment when America's fin de siècle began, might do worse than to point to the glittering evening when the Academy of Motion Picture Arts and Sciences declared that the best picture of 1991 was a slasher movie, *Silence of the Lambs*. *Silence* featured not one, but two serial killers, the twisted genius Hannibal Lecter and grunting Buffalo Bill, who murders women with the improbable motive of stitching himself together a female skin. Clarice Starling, a novice FBI agent played by Jodie Foster, represents the law. With the help of Hannibal (and her own dark side), she tracks Buffalo Bill to his lair and blows him away. For his part, Lecter, known popularly as Hannibal the Cannibal, escapes to a remote island, there to continue his pursuit of high culture and anthropophagy.

Around 1975 slasher films began proliferating in America: *Texas Chainsaw Massacre, Halloween, Nightmare on Elm Street, Friday the Thirteenth*. But these were down and dirty productions, shot on shoestring budgets and patronized by adolescents looking for quasi-sexual shivers, and by the sorts of middle-aged men who have trouble keeping eye contact. But then suddenly, at the onset of the '90s, an expensively produced slasher film was at the center of mainstream American culture. Middle America was lining up to enjoy a world where women were flayed and men devoured; where the good, as embodied by Agent Starling, require tutelage from the worst, Lecter; and where the archvillain is left free at the end to follow his singular calling.

Horror had reached prime time—and it has stayed there. During the last decade of the century (and millennium), horror plays a central role in American culture. A time of anxiety, dread about the future, the fin de siècle teems with works of Gothic terror and also with their defensive antidotes, works that summon up, then cavalierly deny, Gothic fears.

The 1990s have seen a boom in horror fiction and film. After *Silence of the Lambs* swept the Academy Awards, Coppola directed *Dracula;* Kenneth Branagh ran pell-mell through *Mary Shelley's Frankenstein;* Jack Nicholson became the wolf-man. Anne Rice has been enthralling readers with her sadomasochistic vampire duo, Louis and Lestat. Stephen King ("I'll try to terrify you first, and if that doesn't work, I'll try to horrify you, and if I can't make it there, I'll try to gross you out. I'm not proud") has trumped all previous Gothic writers, with nearly 250 million books in circulation. His commercial supremacy in the '90s is being challenged by only one American writer, a self-effacing man named R. L. Stine, author of fright novels for adolescents: *The Scarecrow Walks at Midnight, Dead End, Haunted,* and (my own favorite title) *Cheerleaders: The First Evil.* Terror has probably never been so hot, surely never so lucrative.

Most of these productions, whether their creators know it or not, are descendants of the Gothic novel, the terror fiction that took off in England while the French Revolution was unfolding across the Channel. Like the eighteenth-century Gothic best-sellers, Ann Radcliffe's *Mysteries of Udolpho* and Matthew Gregory Lewis's *The Monk,* much of our current horror fare depicts a maiden in distress (sometimes we substitute a child), usually trapped in a horrible ruin (a castle, an abbey, a catacomb). And of course there is the pursuing villain—usually a hero-villain in fact, a split personality with noble qualities as well as base—who embodies the audience's pressing desires and fears. The Gothic of 1790s England seems to have risen up again, specterlike, in 1990s America.

Gothic shows the dark side, the world of cruelty, lust, perversion, and crime that, many of us at least half believe, is hidden beneath established conventions. Gothic tears through censorship, explodes hypocrisies, to expose the world as the corrupted, reeking place it is—or so its proponents maintain.

Unsentimental, enraged by gentility and high-mindedness, skeptical about progress in any form, the Gothic mind is antithetical to all smiling American faiths. A nation of ideals, America has also been, not surprisingly, a nation of hard disillusionment, with a fiercely reactive Gothic imagination. Ours is the culture that produced both "Self-Reliance" and "The Fall of the House of Usher."

Gothic is the art of haunting, and in two senses. Gothic shows time and again that life, even at its most ostensibly innocent, is possessed, that the present is in thrall to the past. All are guilty. All must, in time, pay up. And Gothic also sets out to haunt its audience, possess them so they can think of nothing else. They have to read it—or see it—again and again to achieve some peace. (Repetition, Freud claimed, is the way we attempt to master a trauma.) For a work to be Gothic, the critic Chris Baldick says, it "should combine a fearful sense of inheritance in time with a claustrophobic sense of enclosure in space, these two dimensions reinforcing one another to produce an impression of sickening descent into disintegration."[1] When a culture teems with such work and cannot produce persuasive alternatives, its prognosis is anything but favorable.

It is noteworthy, to be sure, that at century's end fear constitutes one of our most common forms of entertainment. But what is more arresting, and more in need of analysis, is the fact that the conventions of Gothic horror are making their way into, and decisively shaping, many apparently nonfictional forms. On broadcast news, in the most respected daily papers, on TV talk shows, in our modes of therapy (and America is becoming more and more a therapeutic society), in our medical and environmental discourses, and even in advanced brands of intellectual analysis, the Gothic mode is ascendant. Not only do the '90s media seem to seek out Gothic tales to bring to the center of cultural consciousness, they also sometimes rework events until they assume the proper Gothic shape. And though our supposedly nonfictive Gothic productions may deploy plots akin to those of Ann Radcliffe and Monk Lewis (as he liked to be called), their spirit is, in general, much darker and more characteristically American, the legacy of Edgar Allan Poe.

This book begins with a survey and a diagnosis of 1990s American Gothic, but it does not stop there. In the pages to come, I also consider a mode that appears to be entirely antithetical to the Gothic, a mode I call facile transcendence. The ethos of facile transcendence, epitomized as it is by the various New Age panaceas, by the fixation with guardian angels, and by the pervasive attraction to idealized celebrity images, is that you can transform yourself into a higher being with little or no exertion required. I'm reminded of a line by the poet John Hollander: poetry is easy to write if you don't know how.

On the face of it, it would appear that the ethos of facile transcendence has little, if anything, to do with that of the Gothic. But in the second chapter I show how facile, feelgood productions like *Forrest Gump* are in fact significantly related to the ascendancy of Gothic, to terror's reign. Such productions, I believe, defend their consumers against the Gothic—but without ever acknowledging its prowess. They evoke Gothic, then turn blithely, defensively away.

A truly regenerative vision, this book will argue, becomes possible when the Gothic and the visionary or renewing drives confront each other directly, something that has not generally come to pass in fin de siècle American culture. To demonstrate how and why the visionary has successfully confronted the Gothic in the past, it will be necessary to turn back to the movement misleadingly called Romanticism, and show how it is both an art of haunting *and* an art of regeneration. This turning back, which I do in the third chapter, entails offering a new account of the visionary movement (my preferred name for it) and also a redescription of some consequential art and culture of the present. In Toni Morrison's *Beloved* and in Tony Kushner's *Angels in America*, there are attempts, brilliant and moving if not entirely successful, to confront Gothic despair with regenerative visionary force.

Ann Radcliffe and Monk Lewis initiate the first wave of Anglo-American Gothic, which we might call *terror Gothic*. The next great originator after Radcliffe and Lewis is Mary Shelley, who in *Frankenstein* gives us the source for *apocalyptic Gothic*. In this form humanity's past creations or crimes—often, in apocalyptic Gothic, creation *is* crime—explode into the present. In apocalyptic Gothic an outraged Nature seeks revenge. The third innovation comes from a German writer, but his influence in the West has been so large that he transcends national identity. In showing us that our psyches are thoroughly haunted, Sigmund Freud gives us what I call *internalized Gothic*.

Lewis and Radcliffe write in the 1790s; Shelley's *Frankenstein* comes out in 1818; Freud creates the haunted psyche from 1900 to 1939. This chapter describes these three originating forms, shows how they are active today, and speculates on the cultural work they perform. Our premillennial moment is singular, perhaps, in that all three of the major forms of Gothic are currently thriving. "May you live in interesting times," goes an ancient Chinese curse.

First, terror Gothic, a form that stretches from Radcliffe and Lewis to media renderings of the O. J. Simpson case and beyond. In *Mysteries of Udolpho* Radcliffe invented one of Hannibal Lecter's major predecessors, the cruel aristocrat Montoni and, in *The Italian*, the ruthless Schedoni. Both characters owe something to Hamlet (a revenger, after all) and something to

Milton's Satan from *Paradise Lost,* English literature's grand rebel. In *The Monk,* Lewis gave his contemporaries their most disturbing specter, Ambrosio, a celebrated, pious monk who descends to fornication, murder, and incest.

From a contemporary perspective, late-eighteenth-century terror Gothic can look like a bundle of conventions. Besides the tyrannical hero-villain with the piercing glare, there's inevitably a trembling heroine and her impetuous lover, who comes, usually in his sweet time, to save the day; the scene is often an oppressive ruin, surrounded by a wild landscape; the society is Catholic, usually feudal. Certain preoccupations frequently arise: the priesthood and monastic institutions, sleeplike and deathlike states, subterranean spaces and live burials, the uncovering of obscure family ties, possibilities of incest (and sometimes the real thing), Faust- and Wandering Jew–like figures. We encounter civil insurrections and fires, the charnel house and the madhouse. One of the major resources of this Gothic mode is the double. The idea of a second self—of a horrible other living unrecognized within us, or loosed somehow into the world beyond—is central to the vision of terror Gothic and active in the other modes as well.[2]

Surely, says the literary critic Eve Kosofsky Sedgwick, from whose compressed account of Gothic I have been drawing, no modern literary form as influential as terror Gothic is so pervasively conventional. But what look like mere conventions to the literary scholar can be, for the intense reader and the writer possessed by a vision, means of insight. The best terror Gothic woke its eighteenth-century readers up. It roused them from the smug self-assurance often induced by enlightenment rationalism. Gothic was a blow against the sanitized, empirical philosophies of the age. In Gothic novels readers discovered, or were reacquainted with, the night side of life. They met up with fears and desires that enlightened reason had banished. My objective here will be to enquire into what late-twentieth-century terror Gothic does for us.

In the middle of our millennium's final decade, all of America became transfixed by a Gothic slasher production made, it often seemed, for TV. I mean, of course, the O. J. Simpson case. Simpson was habitually cast as an archetypal Gothic hero-villain. He was rendered as a man with a divided nature, intermittently possessed by a demon within.

Newsweek put it this way: "Simpson lived a double life. The corporate spokesman who drank an occasional beer with Hertz executives was also a hard partyer . . . who cruised bars and indulged in drugs and random sex. His wife believed he was a cocaine addict; his friends, who saw him on the prowl at wild parties in Los Angeles, thought his real addiction was white women. The smooth talker took lessons to make his diction more 'white.' The family man was seldom home."[3]

Simpson leads a double life. He's black inside and white outside, to cut through to the magazine's central and repugnant thesis. *Newsweek*'s Simpson is haunted by the needs of his black self. ("Addiction" is one of our contemporary words for haunting, the Gothic state proper, just as "obsession" was one of Freud's.) This motif of the double, of two persons in one, is, as I suggested, essential to the Gothic vision. You can find it in Monk Lewis, with his depiction of Ambrosio, a saint on the surface who nurtures Satan deep inside; in Poe, who makes use of the double theme in most of the major tales; in E. T. A. Hoffmann (from whom Freud learned); in Robert Louis Stevenson's *Doctor Jekyll and Mr. Hyde* and Oscar Wilde's *Picture of Dorian Gray*. The theme is profusely developed by Alfred Hitchcock (a devoted Gothic artist and perhaps the most influential filmmaker of all time), most obviously in *Shadow of a Doubt* and *Strangers on a Train*. But, like the balance of Poe's tales, most of Hitchcock's films play in some way with doubles. For its part, *Time* magazine altered a photo of Simpson for its cover, making him look cruder and more thuggish than we generally envisioned him: Mr. Hyde had emerged.[4]

Depicting O. J. Simpson in terms of the Gothic double wasn't limited to the newsweeklies. It was also a major strategy for the prosecution in the murder trial. District attorney Christopher Darden described Simpson to the jury as follows: "What we've been seeing, ladies and gentlemen, is the public face, the public persona, the face of the athlete, the face of the actor. It is not the actor who is on trial here today, ladies and gentlemen. It is not that public face. Like many public men . . . they have a private side, a private life, a private face. And that is the face we will expose to you in this trial, the other side of O. J. Simpson, the side you never met before . . . When we look upon and look behind that public face . . . you'll see a different face. And the evidence will show that the face you will see and the man that you will see will be the face of a batterer, a wife beater, an abuser, a controller . . . the face of Ron's and Nicole's murderer."[5] The creators of Dorian Gray and Mr. Hyde could surely have said it better than Chris Darden manages to, but in his Gothic premises, Darden is very much the inheritor of Wilde and Stevenson. In the civil case, in which Simpson was charged with damages stemming from wrongful death, the Gothic rhetoric continued on, with the plaintiffs' lawyers determined to expose "the dark side of Mr. Simpson."[6]

The psychological theory of the double is both reductive and powerful. It assumes that we are all playing a role in life, that inside a raving beast waits for the chains to loosen or snap. Doubles stories seem to proliferate when people sense an unnegotiable divide between the true or natural self and society, between nature and culture. From the charisma that Radcliffe confers on Montoni, which invites some measure of reader identification, to the I-camera technique that lets the audience see through the serial killer's eyes in slasher films, Gothic works invite the audience to acquaint themselves with, and to fear, the shadow that dwells within. (Freud, brilliant horror writer that he was, called his version of the shadow the "id"; all of us have an "it," a hungering, formless, ungendered thing, living within us.) The premise of Gothic's double psychology is that we ought to be very afraid—and of nothing so much as ourselves.

No Gothic narrative can work unless the villain is in some way an admirable figure. "He is the *animus* regarded as forgivable victim of passion and circumstance, as admirable sufferer," writes Leslie Fiedler. "His brow furrowed, his face frozen in the grimace of pain, his eyes burning with repressed fury, his mind tormented with unspeakable blasphemies," the Gothic hero-villain of Lewis and Radcliffe is, Fiedler observes, the ancestor of Byron's Giaour, of Ahab, Heathcliffe, Rochester, and a thousand other "ungodly godlike" men. So too, we might add, is that Gothic hero-villain incarnated as the media's O. J. Simpson and many of his supposedly newsworthy contemporaries.[7]

O. J. Simpson, true to his terror-Gothic role, pursues a woman who, again in the words of Fiedler, the best literary critic of the Gothic, escapes her terrible persecutor, "who seek[s] her out of lust and greed, but is caught; escapes again and is caught; escapes once more and is caught."[8] But Simpson's case isn't Radcliffe's *Mysteries of Udolpho;* the unfortunate heroine doesn't finally break free and marry her earnest, honest love. Simpson's is a terror Gothic tale with a brutal close.

Like a Radcliffe novel, the Simpson tale is a mystery. Though unlike the mysteries surrounding Castle Udolpho, which Mrs. Radcliffe assiduously clears up down to the last detail (that bloody corpse was just a waxwork), those that have arisen from the Simpson case may never get their resolution. It is mystery, suspense, that keeps one fixed on the Gothic—and that will, despite the verdicts, probably keep America fixed on Simpson until well into the future.

One of the common functions of the Gothic is to turn anxiety, the vague but insistent fear of what will happen in the future, into suspense. The Gothic novel or film in effect gathers up the anxiety that is free-floating in the reader or viewer and binds it to a narrative. Thus the anxiety is displaced and brought under temporary, tenuous control. If anxiety is, as is so often said, a preeminent fin-de-siècle emotion, and if the Gothic can deliver some qualified relief from anxiety's pressures, then it is no surprise that our moment is rife with Gothic forms. The Simpson case was, perhaps, a national occasion for the transformation of free-floating anxiety into suspense. Our obsessive fascination with the case may stem in part from a drive for a conclusion—some final answers—that will let the anxiety be discharged, at least for a while.

As to locale, surely there were Radcliffean mansions enough for the horrors of the Simpson case, from beatings to murder, to transpire in. And one might wager that Los Angeles is, to channel-scanning America, as weirdly foreign a place, as pagan and elemental, as Roman Catholic Italy and Spain were to British readers of the 1790s. If Washington, D.C., is America's superego (at least ideally), then Los Angeles is the national id, glamorous, gaudy, decadent.

Even had Simpson not been available, there were many other candidates in the news who could have taken his central terror-Gothic role. One thinks of the Unabomber, the mysterious figure who killed for an obscure political program, or of Timothy McVeigh, guilty of the bombing of the Oklahoma Federal Building and depicted as a fanatical, right-wing extremist, fired by ideals, though ideals of the worst sort. These figures lack the aura of the grand terror-Gothic villain—they aren't mysterious enough, complex enough; they don't embody enough ostensibly elevated values for their corruption to be of consequence. Though touted as a "Twisted Genius" on the cover of *U.S. News and World Report* and as a "Mad Genius" on the cover of *Time,* purported Unabomber Theodore Kaczynski was probably too grubby in appearance and too complex in his motives for prolonged stardom. But perhaps saying as much is to underestimate the current media: perhaps it would have been possible to modify the profiles of even such unpromising candidates as McVeigh and Kaczynski and to make them work.

More ready to hand for '90s Gothic has been the image of Michael Jackson luring young boys into his pre-adolescent pleasure dome for frolic and friendship. Jackson—the male-female, child-adult, black-white, waif-mogul, and most centrally the presexual sexual predator—has been readily depicted in terms of the Gothic double. What he lacks is O. J.'s élan and his menace. It is hard to make an aristocratic hero-villain out of a gorgeously lit lounge act.

Also abiding in the wings has been the specter of the serial killer, the Jeffrey Dahmers and Ted Bundys, whom writers like Norman Mailer and Joyce Carol Oates have encouraged us to see as emblematic of our cultural moment. To Mailer, they are the just reward for our alienating social arrangements. We move around too much, sacrificing community and belonging for new possibilities in faraway places. With all the migration, we tend not to know our neighbors, or care much about them. Serial killers can slip in and out undetected.

Oates's 1995 novel *Zombie* is narrated by the serial murderer Quentin P——, whose life's objective is to lobotomize a few young men (with an ice pick) and so create a tribe of zombies to love and serve him.[9] Quentin revels in junk food and mainlines TV. He's high on one thing or another whenever possible, America's lowest-common-denominator man. Has our culture, Oates prods us to ask, created Quentin, in something of the way that Quentin would create zombies from the unhappy young men he picks up on the roadside and in gay bars? From the perspective of Oates's Gothic novel, the serial killer might simply be America incarnate.

For those who would have taken some satisfaction in reading Lewis's *The Monk*, there has been an endless run of stories about priests molesting young children, most often boys. There came the Menendez brothers, whose defense against the charge of killing their parents pushed the eighteenth-century terror-Gothic plot a step further. (A mansion figured in this one, too.) The pair, their defense attorneys claimed, were victimized; and, fighting back in the manner of Gothic heroines, they purportedly dispatched their specters, their molesters (their parents). We encountered Susan Smith, who claimed that a black man had driven off with her children. Then, finally, she confessed to their drowning. For weeks America was riveted, first in sympathy, then rage. "Southern Gothic on Trial" ran *Newsweek*'s headline.[10]

One recalls John Wayne Bobbitt and his wife Lorena, who severed his penis as revenge for purported abuse. Once America's first Gothic family, the Bobbitts eventually became just a sporadically visible sideshow. John appeared in a few porn movies to testify to modern medicine's prowess and his own. Lorena's name pops up occasionally in feminist tracts, where she plays the role of Gothic heroine-villainess capably enough.

In the mid-1980s the McMartin Preschool molestation case was a mainstay of the evening news. Children averred that they had been taken up in airplanes and brought on board submarines to be molested. There were also Satanic rituals in churches and graveyards, animal sacrifices, and blood-quaffing. Teachers flew naked on broomsticks. No one was found guilty, though the McMartin family played the role of debauched clan to all of America for five years. In Wes Craven's 1977 film *The Hills Have Eyes* the wacko mountain family sets after the lost city folk with the design of killing the men, raping the women, and eating the baby. Soon one didn't need to turn to shock horror films to encounter a comparable plot.

In a less bizarre register there was the Nancy Kerrigan–Tonya Harding episode, which TV and newspapers used some ingenuity to work into a Gothic tale of opposing twins. Harding, who was accused of arranging an assault on Kerrigan, her figure-skating rival, was quickly cast as a heroine-villainess (in eighteenth-century Gothic a role that was often taken by debauched, sadistic mothers superior). Tonya was quirky, libidinal, spooked, a trailer-park bitch; Nancy was an American princess. The fact that the two young women, both working class, both ambitious and talented, neither oppressively bright, had more in common than not was erased by the need for a certain sort of story, another Gothic doubles tale.

A decade or so ago, these stories—O. J., Michael Jackson, John and Lorena, Nancy and Tonya, and many others like them—would have been relegated to the back pages of all but the sleaziest newspapers. But in the 1990s the Gothic melodramas have come up front, presented, often implicitly, as objects of cultural haruspicy, hot entrails for the audience to puzzle over so as to divine where society has gone and why.

Most of the central figures that I have been describing in these accounts of '90s terror Gothic are not just villains, but hero- (or heroine-) villains. To be a Gothic antagonist, a character has to embody some measure of the good, even if it is a specious good. It matters that Simpson is a rich man and a star athlete, a purported role model; that Tonya Harding is a prize skater; that the molester is a respected priest; that Michael Jackson wishes to be known for his "We Are the World" largesse; that Montoni is a nobleman; Ambrosio a powerful, commissioned soldier in the army of Christ. The serial killer, as described by Mailer and Oates and rendered by Oliver Stone in *Natural Born Killers*, isn't merely a sadistic thug, but just retribution for our creating an estranging, brutal society. Fin-de-siècle culture has invented the serial killer as avenging angel, society's scourge.

Even the monsters who rise up in slasher films, Freddy Krueger, Michael Myers, and Jason, are, as Carol Clover notes in her brilliant study of the genre, monsters of morality, enforcing a certain ethic.[11] To put it inelegantly, they kill the kids who copulate, or want to. Whenever you see two young people about to frolic in a slasher film, you know that within minutes they will be sliced, macheted, garrotted, pierced with an arrow, a spear, a pitchfork—whatever is handy, sharp, and primitive enough to evoke primal punishment. In slasher films, there are no *petites morts*.

Howling in the background of all slasher movies is Mrs. Bates, from Alfred Hitchcock's *Psycho*, the first of the genre's moral monsters. Before Marion Crane takes her famous shower, Norman Bates invites her to come up to the house for some dinner. But when Norman's mother hears about her son's plan, she goes berserk. "Tell her," Mrs. Bates rages to Norman (within whose psyche she uncomfortably resides), "she will not be appeasing her ugly appetite with my food or my son."

Freddy Krueger of *Nightmare on Elm Street*, like Mrs. Bates, who had a lover, is a libidinous character. He sends a raunchy purple tongue through the telephone to French kiss the film's heroine, Nancy (a sublime piece of cheapo special effects). In his mortal incarnation, before he began stalking the Elm Street kids in their dreams, he was, it seems, a child molester. He has a prehensile tongue disposed to miming cunnilingus. Freddy, in other words, punishes what he also seems to enjoy and enjoin. And this paradox is at the center of the Gothic vision, both in the late twentieth century and at its origins. The terror-

Gothic figure who announces in stentorian tones that Thou shalt not, himself does, and does, and does.

The first big wave of American slasher movies ran from about 1975 to the late 1980s, until the genre went mainstream and expensive with *Silence of the Lambs*. Then in 1994 Wes Craven, director of *Nightmare on Elm Street*, issued *Wes Craven's New Nightmare*, a film that was about its own making, a modernist film in Stanley Cavell's terms, in that it took itself, its own origins and possibilities, as its subject: Bertolt Brecht meets the horror flick. And it failed miserably. It's a silly, derivative movie, so imaginatively barren that it's forced to steal scenarios from middle-class fright films like *The Omen*.

But *New Nightmare* didn't fail because the vision of Craven's first *Nightmare* no longer had any currency, nor because the many slasher sequels that Hollywood coughed up regularly over a fifteen-year period had succeeded in burning up the genre's possibilities. Craven's later movie was driven to extremes, I suspect, because major aspects of the '70s-'80s horror film had come alive in the world of respectable culture. To compete with that culture, Craven in 1994 had to reach toward high art, which he did ineptly enough. His proper territory—shock horror—had been appropriated. Why watch *New Nightmare* on HBO when the Simpson case, a true-life slasher story, was on the other channel? If an avant-garde cultural form is one that has been able to predict—not necessarily influence, but predict—the direction of much that comes later, then the slasher films, of which Craven's first *Nightmare* and Tobe Hooper's *Texas Chainsaw Massacre* are among the most inspired examples, must qualify: they went a long way to foretelling major tendencies in upcoming culture.

Early terror Gothic was the literature of revolution. This much the Marquis de Sade clearly perceived. De Sade, purported inventor of sadism, professed himself a deep admirer of both Lewis and Radcliffe. Their kind of fiction, Sade observed, was "the inevitable result of the revolutionary shocks which all of Europe has suffered. For anyone familiar with the full range of misfortunes wherewith evildoers can beset mankind, the novel became as difficult to write as monotonous to read. There was not a man alive who had not experienced in the short span of four or five years more misfortunes than the most celebrated novelist could portray in a century. Thus, to compose works of interest, one had to call upon the aid of hell itself, and to find in the world of make-believe things wherewith one was fully familiar merely by delving into man's daily life in this age of iron."[12]

But it was the conservative Edmund Burke, not the self-described revolutionary de Sade, who put a vision of revolution and terror at the disposal of the English Gothic writers. (We might think of Burke as the founder of political Gothic, a mode of terror Gothic, as I see it.) In the 1790 *Reflections on the Revolution in France*, Burke develops a rhetoric of Gothic monstrosity to capture what he takes to be the excesses of the French people in rebellion against their anointed king. Burke speaks of France as devolving into a "military democracy; a species of political monster which has always ended by devouring those who have produced it."[13]

The first Gothic heroine, it has been said, is Burke's Marie Antoinette—woman on the run through the halls of Versailles, revolutionary vengeance following close on her heels. "A band of cruel ruffians and assassins, reeking with . . . blood, rushed into the chamber of the queen, and pierced with an hundred strokes of bayonets and poniards the bed, from whence this persecuted woman had but just time to fly almost naked, and through ways unknown to the murderers had escaped to seek refuge at the feet of a king and husband, not secure of his own life for a moment."[14]

Almost naked: how many times would this scene be written and rewritten over the next decade in England? Before Lewis and Radcliffe, there was the example of Horace Walpole's *Castle of Otranto,* much read and little imitated. And surely one might find virtually every Gothic convention somewhere in Shakespeare. (One of the reasons, I suspect, that the so-called Romantic period embraced *Hamlet,* and that we ourselves tend to see it at the center of the Shakespeare canon, is that it is his most Gothic work.) But it wasn't until the revolutionary age that Sade describes that the floodgates opened and hundreds of books came forth, books with titles like *Deeds of Darkness, or The Unnatural Uncle; Gondez the Monk; The Demon of Sicily; The Invisible Enemy, or the Mines of Wielitska;* and, from an ancestor of today's film-sequel creators, a Lewis-Radcliffe amalgam, *The Monk of Udolpho.*[15]

But perhaps the greatest Gothic political writer—greater even than the arch-conservative Burke—was Karl Marx. In effect, Marx took the rhetoric that Burke had used against the people and sent it in two directions. "A specter is haunting Europe," begins *The Communist Manifesto,* and that specter is of course communism: Marx in effect accepts Burke's insulting terms for the people in revolt and uses them to try to frighten the bourgeoisie.

Yet he also turns the Gothic idiom against the oppressors. Marx's favorite Gothic trope is vampirism. He writes that British industry, vampire-like, lives by sucking blood, and children's blood at that. On another occasion the bourgeoisie is said to have become a hoary vampire that sucks out the peasants' blood and brains and "throws them into the alchemist's cauldron of capital." For Marx, as Chris Baldick says, capital is accumulated, or dead, labor; the capitalist preys on the living, turning their energy and life force into inert property, just as the vampire takes living blood and uses it to perpetuate his death in life.[16]

Political Gothic entails finding the dark self, the double, that lurks inside your brightly shining adversary, then making your audience see that and only that. Capitalists look like heroes, captains of industry: in reality they're a gang of bloodsuckers. Vampires are always aristocrats, and by associating the capitalists with the vampire legends, Marx implies that the old nobility that we thought we'd gotten rid of is still with us. So drive the stake through once more, sever the head, burn the corpse.

Terror Gothic is an ideal idiom for expressing political rancor, and the 1990s has witnessed a good deal of it. Bill Clinton, who wishes to come off as earnest, responsible, and trustworthy, has become, to many in America, Montoni incarnate, if not Freddy Krueger. One can learn the Gothic truth about the 42nd president of the United States in *The Clinton Chronicles*, a samizdat video that has sold more than half a million copies. *The Clinton Chronicles* purports to show that Clinton has been a heavy cocaine user, a philanderer far beyond what we commonly imagine, the aider and abettor of an international drug ring, and the mastermind of a criminal conspiracy responsible for multiple murders.

Clinton, in his terror-Gothic guise, is said to have covered up the killing of his friend Vincent Foster. He schemes constantly against public morals. His mother—a slightly subdued version of Stephen King's crazed Nurse Annie of *Misery* fame—was responsible for a sequence of hospital deaths. He is married to Lady Macbeth. To many people there are two Bill Clintons, the affable if wishy-washy character who presides at press conferences and affairs of state, and the shadow-self, the double: a monster out to destroy America.

Gothic thrives in a world where those in authority—the supposed exemplars of the good—are under suspicion. The mind of terror Gothic senses hypocrisy in high places. But it is also fascinated by heights, by power, position, fame. It requires contact with glamour to keep its spirits up, yet mistrusts the fascination on which it compulsively feeds. It seeks absolute stability and assurance from leaders, and then rebels when the leaders are revealed as fallible and not fully in charge, or (worse yet) when they really do succeed in establishing complete control. A deep ambivalence about authority lies near the heart of our culture of Gothic.

There is also a Gothic George Bush. Bush, even in retirement, is supposed to be close to the center of something called the New World Order, a group of plotters devoted to handing over the United States to a federated world government. (In Texas there are Soviet tanks.) Bush started the Gulf War in order to enrich his own family, which had extensive holdings in Kuwait. (There are black helicopters hidden all over America.)

With the Oklahoma bombing, America was exposed to a panoply of right-wing conspiracy theories, stuff about federated Jewish bankers and a plot to bring the United States under the control of the United Nations, dividing it into regional departments (dissolving the states); fantasies about the Hong Kong police and microchips that hospitals routinely implant under their patients' skin; mutterings about a program to turn the weather into a weapon of mass destruction. Such beliefs are part of the proper terror-Gothic orientation (though they surely have other affiliations as well), which insists that there is always something rotten at the top, especially when the leaders are devoted to parading their virtues. Paranoia is sanity: what you don't know will hurt you; what you do know probably will, too.

The post-Oklahoma-bombing news stories that sought to describe the supposedly widespread right-wing militia movements kept on interviewing the same person, the eloquent if rather deranged John Trochmann. Surely there are others who share Trochmann's views, but media renderings of the militia-world suggest these types to be far more plentiful than they are. In effect, such renderings helped to create the view, held by many reasonable citizens, that there is a host of conspiracy-finding conspirators out there, a vast world that serves as a dark double to the visible everyday world. What emerged from these extensive portraits of the militias was what one might call a second-order political Gothic, not as vivid as the primary version sustained by the likes of Trochmann, but still productive of an essential terror-Gothic emotion, paranoia.

But I'm not sure I want to say that instances of political Gothic are *always* hyped productions. For there was Richard Nixon. Nixon—to me, anyway—simply *was* a Gothic hero-villain, very light on the hero. (Note that Anthony Hopkins won plaudits *first* as Hannibal Lecter in *Silence of the Lambs*, *then* as Nixon in the Oliver Stone version of the great man's life.) When the mad bomber of Cambodia gets on his knees late at night in a haunted White House and begins talking to the portraits of former presidents, we are with Monk Lewis and Horace Walpole. (Paintings in terror Gothic are forever coming to life.) In *The Public Burning*, his novel based on the Rosenberg case, Robert Coover seems determined to offer an over-the-top depiction of Nixon as Gothic villain. But he is unable to invent much that passes beyond the mere reality. It's Clinton's aspiration to come off as something of a secular angel that makes him so susceptible to Gothic slander; Nixon was self-Gothicized enough to make further efforts superfluous.

The point I want to make about the instances of real-life Gothic I have been describing isn't that they rest on rank falsifications. Renderings of the Simpson case, the Michael Jackson debacle, and the rest have some relation to actual events; something happened. But such events are far rarer than current media would lead us to think. (It's instructive, perhaps, that three of our most influential horror films—*Psycho*, *The Texas Chainsaw Massacre*, and *Silence of the Lambs*—were all based on the life of the same serial killer, a Wisconsin farmer named Ed Gein.) What matters is the way the instances I have recounted have been cast, with more or less distortion involved, into a terror-Gothic idiom, and then—this point matters most—understood to be at the center of the culture. They are taken to be summaries, the keys to the deep truth about America.

But terror Gothic is not the only Gothic form active in American culture today: we are also responding to purportedly nonfiction versions of *apocalyptic Gothic,* a mode in many ways invented by Mary Shelley. Apocalyptic Gothic is collective Gothic: as terror Gothic would haunt the individual, so exercises in apocalyptic Gothic would haunt the society at large. The vision that affirms that when we usurp nature's role, especially through technology, what we create will turn on us, punishing us for our hubris, is first and most memorably rendered in Shelley's 1818 novel, *Frankenstein.* From there it becomes a major element of Gothic mythmaking. In *Frankenstein* the gloom-drenched laboratory full of ominous equipment replaces the haunted castle; the possessed scientist plays the role of hero-villain (the monster in many ways is his double); victims are multiple: women and children and innocent men go first, but ultimately the creator himself often has to pay the full price.

With the demise of the former Soviet Union, apocalyptic Gothic, which was often associated with nuclear threat, has declined. (A brilliant essay by Susan Sontag, "The Imagination of Disaster," subtly shows the degree to which nuclear fear invested the many science-fiction films of the 1950s and '60s.)[17] Apocalyptic Gothic is also the most commonly hybridized of Gothic forms: crimes against nature are, to cite just one example, easily seen as crimes against the deity. (Mary

Shelley's book, though, is emphatically secular.) One might confidently predict that as the millennium nears, apocalyptic broodings will become more common and more intense, and that they will continue to exploit Gothic terms. Yet even in the mid-1990s there are important cultural discourses in which apocalyptic Gothic metaphors hold sway.

Everyone knows the Frankenstein story, though only those who have read Shelley's novel are likely to know that the scientist's name is Frankenstein and that the living thing he stitches together from graveyard refuse is nameless: he's simply "the creature." The creature begins life as a surpassingly sensitive being, a Rousseauian child of nature. It's only after being repeatedly humiliated, rebuffed, and mistreated by humanity in general and his maker in particular that the creature runs amok.

By usurping nature's generative powers, Victor Frankenstein makes himself an outcast, one who suffers nature's wrath. Nature's, not God's: like terror Gothic, apocalyptic Gothic begins as a secular form. Though Mary Shelley revised her book, publishing a version in 1831 that was more acceptable to orthodox tastes, the first edition posits the natural order as the ultimate authority, which is part of what made the book so terrifying and distasteful to many of its first readers.

Frankenstein came out of a competition among Mary; her husband, Percy Bysshe Shelley, possibly the greatest lyric poet in English; Lord Byron, the best-known poet of the day; and Byron's personal physician, the comprehensively inept John Polidori. While still in her teens, she wrote what may be the most powerful modern myth in Anglo-American literature.

Yet the book itself is in many ways unsatisfying. It's as though someone won the lottery and kept changing her mind about how to spend the winnings. There are so many directions to take once you've hit on the basic idea—a man made by a man—that it's hard to surrender any of them, and Mary

Shelley doesn't. The novel is about mankind (the creature) facing an uncomprehending god (Victor Frankenstein); about the corrupting power of society (a standard theme of the period); about the perils of repression, with the monster playing the role of Victor's murderous unconscious; about the artist and his work of art, taking on, as the saying goes, a life of its own: one could add more.

But Hollywood, with multiple productions of the story to its credit, has come on to save the day, reducing the work, but in doing so effectively intensifying it, too. The scene we all remember from almost every production of *Frankenstein*, beginning with the 1931 Boris Karloff–James Whale triumph, is the one in which, storm roaring outside, the machinery clatters and bangs, steam rises, and lightning comes rippling through the wires. Cut to the creature, lying stone still on the laboratory table. Nothing, nothing, nothing. Then the slightest hint of a movement. A drowsy gesture, another. It's alive, alive, and soon out to destroy the human race, or however much of it can be grasped between its strangling hands in the space of sixty or so film minutes.

To Hollywood the Frankenstein story, whatever Mary Shelley might have thought, is all about the dangers of technology and mad professors who sin against nature, competing with its generative prowess. More broadly, of course, the target is humanity, competing with Mother Nature when we should stand in awe.

Mary Shelley's Frankenstein, directed by Kenneth Branagh, who seems to spend the balance of the film running rampant and shirtless in all directions, has, for all its frantic, crescendo-expanding pace, a freshly intelligent variation to make on the myth. When the creature (Robert De Niro) comes to life, he's naked, slipping and sliding in transparent fluids, a newborn baby in his amniotic soup. (Often the monster comes to life in a suit of bad, Eastern-European cut.) Technology in this rendering of the myth is seen as an attempt to wrest the power of parturition from women. They are a useless distraction, and we men could pleasurably conceive a world without them, if only we didn't—and perhaps we won't always—need them for making babies.

The Frankenstein story, as we've come to understand it, is a postreligious rewriting of the fall of mankind, a tragedy in which we overreach and pay for it. The most commercially successful '90s adaptation of the Gothic myth is Steven Spielberg's film *Jurassic Park*. There scientists figure out a way to bring dinosaurs back to life through genetic cloning from prehistoric DNA. (They draw dinosaur blood from an antediluvian mosquito frozen in amber.) But of course humanity isn't meant to create life—a dozen or so speeches by different characters make the point. Someone's going to have to pay for this.

It's all a kind of self-advertisement, of course. For the film is itself doing, with computers, robots, and models, something not unlike what its scientists are doing—creating thunder lizards. *Jurassic Park* gives you, without hubris and at comparatively low cost, what the characters in the film have to suffer Gothic griefs to encounter: dinosaurs, real dinosaurs. Unlike Mary Shelley, however, Spielberg has no wish—it would be counterproductive, against logic and profit—to implicate the audience in the hubris that's being dramatized.

At pay-up time, *Jurassic Park* turns into something of a slasher movie, with an innocent young woman and two children, adept screamers all, careening down corridors, through dark tunnels, and (shades of *The Shining*) in and around a hotel-style kitchen. The pursuing furies are two velociraptors. They're canny beasts who hunt in pairs, rip in with their hooked claws, and begin dining while the prey is still alive. And they don't, the hero insists, look anything like plucked chickens. Hero, played by Sam Neill, carries one of their claws around as a keepsake and gives a little talk on the 'raptors' slashing protocols, so we'll know what's at stake when nature, adapting techniques from Freddy Krueger, decides that payback time has arrived.

In the '90s, apocalyptic Gothic often comes in an ecological mode. Thus one encounters the fear that, as a punishment for human excess, especially of the technological sort, the world is doomed to become a flyblown waste some time in the next decade or two. This scenario divides the field into two parts: the cultural, made up of polluting humanity and all of its institutions and works, and the natural, the once-pristine world. Nature, despoiled and outraged by humanity's wrongs, turns from the sweet nurse described by Wordsworth and Rousseau into a decaying, foul monster seeking vengeance.

So one hears dire prophecies about a dead planet, or more subtle reflections, such as those offered by Bill McKibben, on the end of nature, which maintain that there is no region of the earth to be found now that is not contaminated by culture, slowly dying of the disease that is humanity.[18] More patient and inclusive ecological reflections, in which mankind is recognized as itself from and always in some measure within nature—and indeed the nature-culture opposition is called into some doubt—have no place in such Manichean fables, where all middle terms and qualifications drop away. Apocalyptic environmentalists would rather talk about technological crime and natural punishment than about solutions. Indeed, apocalyptic Gothic is a rhetorical opportunity. Entering into its logic, one can suspend qualifications and enjoy the high provided by a flat-out moralizing rant.

The conviction that nature (tricked out by pseudosecular moralists to look like the Old Testament God) is ripped and looking for retribution is manifest in '90s discourses on diseases and plagues. Gothic motifs turn up in films such as *Outbreak* and *Species*, as well as in news reports about Ebola, an illness that seems to be fatal nearly 100 percent of the time, but that also is not overwhelmingly difficult to guard against. In the public mythology, plagues tend to originate in Africa, a view that may represent guilt for the misery—much of it Western-sponsored—that supposedly prevails throughout that continent.

But most disturbing is the discourse of AIDS, surely our major public occasion for indulgence in apocalyptic Gothic. And AIDS does lend itself readily to Gothic depictions. It's a condition that inhabits its victims, haunts them, often for more than a decade before making itself manifest. It is associated with some act in the distant past, often a socially stigmatized act. The cultural availability of the Gothic plot makes AIDS sufferers easier to demean than they would have been without it. They become the objects of a well-deserved curse for past crimes committed against nature and propriety.

In the Gothic world view, every crime is punished: you can run, but not hide. Susan Sontag captures the compatibility between AIDS and the Gothic idiom when she describes the effect the epidemic must inevitably have on post-AIDS sex. "The fear of AIDS imposes on an act whose ideal is an experience of pure presentness (and a creation of the future) a relation to the past to be ignored at one's peril. Sex no longer withdraws its partners, if only for a moment, from the social sphere: It cannot be considered just a coupling; it is a chain, a chain of transmission, from the past."[19] "A fearful sense of inheritance in time," Baldick noted, lies at the center of the Gothic view.[20] (Yet in the 1989 film *The Fly*, a remake of the 1958 Vincent Price horror movie, one sees how Gothic transformation—human into insect, the animal within—can also be sensitively employed to render the sorrows wrought by the immune deficiency virus.)

Pat Buchanan, once and future presidential candidate, puts the apocalyptic Gothic take on AIDS in compressed terms: "The poor homosexuals," he wrote in 1983, "they have declared war against nature, and now nature is exacting an awful retribution."[21] Camille Paglia too avers that AIDS is nature's revenge for a gay sexual excess that overleaped all natural limits. When she says as much, her thinking is being appropriated—and deformed—by the apocalyptic Gothic idiom.[22]

Paglia is, in fact, the most devotedly Gothic cultural critic currently at work: part of the genius of her remarkable book *Sexual Personae* lies in the way that it locates Gothic elements, particularly death infatuation, in even such apparently upbeat writers as Emerson and Whitman. Part of the book's weakness lies in Paglia's inability to find much that's not Gothic in art from the late eighteenth century to the present.[23]

The instances of apocalyptic Gothic that I have noted entail serious issues: it is one thing to be obsessed by environmental decay, something else to be mesmerized by the fiction of the serial killer as an avenging angel. Yet when the discourses of environmentalism or of AIDS make the Gothic turn, and stay on that road—when they become formulaic horror stories—the result is passivity and fear. Motives for political action or for scientific research can disappear beneath waves of Gothic paranoia.

Comprehensively informing the fin-de-siècle culture of apocalyptic Gothic is the religious fundamentalists' belief in a very real and impending apocalypse. To the premillennarian fundamentalists, we are in the midst of a dark dispensation; the present age is ruled by Satan, the lord of this world. A grand catastrophe now impends. There will be war and tribulation. But at the end of the period of strife, and preliminary to the final judgment, will come a thousand-year reign of peace and harmony. Belief in such prophecies is remarkably common in America (Ronald Reagan, cheerful as he generally was, often spoke the premil language) and surely buttresses all of our more secular forms of apocalyptic fantasy.

Perhaps the most influential apocalyptic-Gothic production in 1990s American culture is nothing other than the evening news, the anchor man our well-groomed, tranquil guide to the terrors of the day. It's on the news that we learn to fear the serial killer, the molester, the abuser, the psychopath, the mad bomber, nuclear disaster, environmental catastrophe, and all of the other Gothically rendered dangers. It's on the news that the diverse images of Gothic coalesce into a world view. Safe shock, as Edmund Burke taught, can be a form of aesthetic experience: Burke associated it with the sublime. The actual experience of TV horror may be safe enough, but the result of an ongoing stream of such stuff is to hardwire anxiety into the populace. TV news is low-grade shock fare, but its long-term effect allows one to see it within the context of apocalyptic Gothic.

Frequently our fin-de-siècle news comprises a sequence of shock footage, a collection of horror shorts. Anywhere around the globe where something terrifying is happening, there the cameras go, whether it is New York or Lebanon or Somalia. Local TV news gives over more than 50 percent of its air-time, on average, to covering crime and disaster.[24] As a *Harper's Magazine* panelist put it, "The alienating engine that I perceive in society is broadcast media, particularly television . . . The reason people are hermetically sealed in their homes is that they are worshipping the glass tit of fear, which is telling them that the world is too scary to go out in."[25] And if the TV news doesn't give you enough, you can catch the panoply of news-horror shows that follow it: true police-stories, true rescue-tales, documentaries about every crime, tragedy, sorrow, disease, mistreatment, humiliation, and loss under the postmodern sun.

New York City—Gotham, if you like—has been transformed by the national news into a terror zone, a city out of

Blade Runner. To travel there is to assume an odds-on chance of torture and disembowelment on day one. A transit policeman, aware of the need to keep up appearances, once asked me, as we watched a parade of happy Midwesterners troop through Grand Central Station, "Why doesn't somebody go mug those people?"

In fact the fin-de-siècle culture of Gothic is inconceivable without the culture of current TV. Marshall McLuhan famously claimed that TV was a cool medium: it was lulling, low-key, and allowed spectators to immerse themselves in the viewing experience, to get mellow and lost. But the medium has changed: now TV is often hot. With 140 channels and a remote control you can fly through the images, creating your own montage effect, turning the former sedative into an amphetamine run.

Quick-cut commercial editing has modified our sensory expectations for TV, accelerating our perceptual capacities and making us receptive to more stimulation. Television can now convey violence more fluently than before: the quick slash, the flying body, the sophisticated dreams of mayhem that made Sam Peckinpah look to some like a cinematic innovator on the order of Sergei Eisenstein are all now within the medium's standard range. And too the breakup of the network monopoly has bred new stations diving ever deeper to find the elusive lowest common denominator. The majors have followed them down.

One disaster succeeds another on apocalyptic news—and because we wish it to be so. The ratings prove as much. We need, it seems, to be frightened, haunted, scared into a stupor.

But wait. Isn't there a very good reason for the proliferation of Gothic in the American 1990s? Isn't it the simple truth that our culture has become more Gothic or, to put it in slightly more sophisticated terms, that the explosion of violence, mayhem, and craziness that the nation has witnessed over the past few years can reasonably be represented by recourse to the Gothic idiom?

No, not really. Since 1991, since the year that *Silence of the Lambs'* Academy Awards sweep signaled a Gothic upsurge, America has actually been becoming a more secure place to live. Since 1991, the Justice Department tells us, the murder rate in America has dropped by 16.3 percent. The rate of violent crime overall is down by nearly 10 percent. We are still far too violent a nation, granted. But the fact remains that while the national consciousness has grown more obsessed with Gothic horror, the national reality has grown more and more stable. Gothic is, in at least one sense, out of step with the facts.

———

Apocalyptic and terror Gothic render haunting as an external phenomenon: you can (sometimes) outrun the hero-villain. Sigmund Freud's ego—his version of the Gothic heroine—has, alas, nowhere to run: the forces that pursue it are also within the psyche. For Freud, the psyche, however else he may describe it, is centrally the haunted house of terror Gothic. Freud's remarkable achievement is to have taken the props and passions of terror Gothic—hero-villain, heroine, terrible place, haunting—and to have relocated them inside the self.

What haunts the psyche? Its traumatic past, and particularly the past relations with parents. From 1900, when he publicly formulated the Oedipus complex, Freud believed that desire for the mother and fear of the father's wrath are at the core of human identity. But because of repression, we can never be aware of how our Oedipal crisis transpired or its day-to-day impact during our adult lives. Past traumas live on in the self, Freud believed, to the point where we can quite literally become possessed, repeating the past in ever-intensifying neurotic circles. When Freud says that we are all sick, he means that we are all chained to the past. Some are chained so tightly that they can barely move; others have a few yards' circumference in which to exercise and take their pleasures. The exorcism that will free us from abnormal bondage to that past Freud calls psychoanalytic therapy.

The psychoanalytical terms that evoke haunting—far too archaic a word for Freud the scientist to employ—include obsession, neurosis, compulsion, repetition, the uncanny, repression, death drive, psychosis. Indeed at least half the glowing words in the Freudian lexicon convey the power of the past to dominate the present.

Freud, in his most resolutely Gothic moods, believed that we never forget anything, so that every past moment is stored somewhere in the psyche. He also thought, at least at times, that *any* negative event that befalls us—no matter how apparently contingent—is in some measure the result of our guilty need for punishment, our wish to self-destruct. Edgar Allan Poe's darkest works, which are glossed by Freud with embarrassing ease, share a similar sense of inevitable doom: the psyche as pit, the ego fearing and desiring the whetted pendulum's blade. In Freud, our inner lives are haunted, but so too is external life. This is so because even the healthiest of us repeat our old traumas with mother and father when we encounter objects of love and objects of authority in the present.

But Freud did more than provide an unremittingly Gothic version of the past; he also succeeded in haunting Victorian culture's most sacrosanct region: he haunted infancy. To the great mass of Freud's Victorian readers, infants were diapered cherubim who came trailing clouds of glory. Their hearts were snowflake. But Freud saw it differently: children were actually more sexually attuned than the adults who defended their virtue. Infants, for Freud, are paragons of sexual response, Blakean experience incarnate. They are, at least potentially, polymorphous perverts. That is, they are able to feel sexual excitation everywhere in their bodies, as though they were one large sexual organ. It's only with socialization (that is, repression) that eros is exiled to certain specific zones—anus, mouth, genitals. Until repression, children are possessed by sex.

Freud was inclined to overplay the resistance he got to his theories. Seeing himself as an embattled outcast effectively energized him. But on one matter, he truly was excoriated. After Freud published his *Three Essays on the Theory of Sexuality* in 1905, with its chapter on infant eroticism, respectable people in Vienna do seem to have crossed the street when they saw him coming their way.

And of course we still live with Freud's perceptions about the hypersexualized child. Informing many of the 1990s scandals about pedophilia is a fear that children really are sexually attuned, sometimes even predatory, and a wish to hide that perception by foisting the blame on adults. Marina Warner has suggested that our culture vacillates between perceptions of children as little angels and as little monsters. We jump from Dickens (at his most sentimental) to Freud and back again, unable to find a more calibrated, more nuanced view.[26] Wanting to have it all one way, to know childhood cold, we've reduced our perceptions to a play between facile idealizations about the child and reactive Gothicism.

In 1914, Freud began to concoct his masterpiece of inward Gothic: the sadistic superego (about which I will have more to say in the last chapter). The sadistic superego is Freud's hero-villain, and I believe the most brilliantly drawn exemplar of that archetype in the entire Gothic tradition. When the figure comes to fruition in the 1930 masterwork, *Civilization and Its Discontents*, we are faced with something truly remarkable.

The superego, according to Freud, is society's garrison within the individual. Installed with the father's Oedipal prohibition, the superego begins as a harsh guide and protector for the child. But, Freud tells us, the superego almost never matures: in most cases it treats us as though we were forever children, demanding the renunciation of pleasures that it would only do the ego good to indulge.

How does the superego grow so fierce? It does so by inhibiting the aggressive energy that comes as part of our biological legacy, there for the preservation of the species. But it not only inhibits the aggression that, brought into full play, would result in the war of each against all. The superego also turns the aggression back on the ego as punishment. And because the superego is, as Freud insists, omniscient, it can punish the hapless ego for crimes it only conceives, never commits. A sadistic hero-villain confining the victim-ego in the haunted precincts of the psyche: we're back in the realms of terror Gothic.

But what makes the superego a hero-villain? The fact that we do not want to slay it out and out because we fear the consequences. Without inner prohibitions, anarchy would be loosed on the world. And the superego, for those rare individuals who can strive to satisfy it, provides standards for beneficial, civilizing achievement. Tragedy, says Hegel, is the result of facing two antithetical goods: in the case of Freud the two rights that come together to make a wrong are the drives and civilization. At the apogee of his career, which comes when he is well into his seventies and badly ill with cancer of the jaw, Freud gives us a Gothic tragedy.

But, it will be objected, Freud is passé. The man whom W. H. Auden recognized as a pervading climate, the cultural weather in which we pursue our individual destinies, has been surpassed, forgotten, proved wrong. From this verdict I depart. Freudian internalized Gothic is alive and well in a number of cultural registers: in therapy (even of many purportedly anti-Freudian sorts), in the form of thought that has come to be known (rather grandly) as theory, and most significantly in our everyday constructions of experience. We are commonsense Freudians in much the way that Chaucer's contemporaries were commonsense Christians: we quote Freud all the time without saying so, and often without knowing as much.

When you understand a dream as a distorted rendering that hides a wish; when you assume that human character is always a function of conflict; when you pursue the meaning of a slip of the tongue; when you emphasize infant and childhood experience in your sense of how the self is formed; when you speak of self-sabotage or self-punishment; when you recognize strategic forgetting; when you find it natural for siblings to compete, for sons to envy fathers, for mothers to vie with daughters; when you assume that because of the dynamics of repression you can know others better than they can know themselves: then you're working within the Freudian field. Here I want to consider some extreme fin-de-siècle variations on Freudian internal Gothic, offshoots from what Ludwig Wittgenstein called Freud's "powerful mythology."

The 1990s saw the rise of the recovered-memory movement, in which young people all over America, mainly women, began to uncover long-repressed memories of being molested by their fathers, the Gothic villain in the house. The recovered-memory scenario is Freudian, internalized Gothic at its most intense. The hero-villain, the father-molester, haunts the inner life of the child, who cannot remember the incident. What cues her, or the helpful therapist, to the truth is a certain array of symptoms: eating disorders, insomnia, depression, anxiety. The therapist plays the role of rescuer (another Gothic archetype), making the repressed memories manifest, and freeing the patient from the grip of the past.

Child abuse is not uncommon in America. But many researchers, contesting the evidence of the recovered-memory movement, argue quite convincingly that it is exceedingly rare for anyone to recover an actual memory of molestation in therapy. Which does not mean that the therapeutic encounters lack significance for the patients: using a Gothic plot can be a way for individuals to express strong feelings about their lives. It's a way of manifesting the depth of their grief and rage. But the therapists, conditioned in part I suspect by Gothic newspapers, Gothic TV, and Freudian Gothic as well, are unable to see the memories as poetic intensifications of a genuine plight. They take their patients literally. This internalized Gothic plot does not, in all probability, constitute an empirical truth, yet the recovered-memory phenomenon has shredded families and sent people to jail.

Richard Ofshe, a professor of social psychology at the University of California at Berkeley, and journalist Ethan Watters have described what they take to be the all-too-frequent dynamics of the patient-therapist exchange in recovered-memory cases:

> Therapists often find themselves forced to explain why, after the first series of recovered memories, the client's symptoms do not disappear as promised. The easiest answer is to presume that the abuse must have been more serious than originally thought, and that more repressed memories are hidden in the patient's unconscious. As the therapist pushes to find more hidden memories, the client, who is already trained in the process, often comes up with still more accounts of having been abused. A vicious cycle is established. When the new set of memories again do nothing to "cure" the client, most likely leaving him or her even more distraught, the therapist can again suggest that even worse memories lie in the unconscious. Once the patient and the therapist become fully adept at the alchemy that turns imagination into memory-belief, the process often continues until the client's worst fears are forged into memories. What could be more psycho-

logically damaging than being raped by one's father? Having to have his baby. What could be worse than having to give birth to your father's child? Having to kill the child. What could be worse than having to kill a baby? Having to eat the baby after you've killed it. What could be worse than all this? Having to do these things during ritualized worship of the Devil.[27]

Ofshe and Watters' account needs to be enlarged to encompass prevailing trends in the culture. What happens in a number of recovered memory cases, I suspect, is that a literary mythology, an internalized form of terror Gothic, is transferred into the purportedly scientific domain of psychological diagnosis and, more disturbingly, of the courts. The Gothic fiction—or rather our inability to draw a distinction between potentially valuable *literary* overstatement and experiential discourse—has had a direct impact on the lives of at least a million Americans.

In 1988 there arose the Satanic ritual scandals in Olympia, Washington, a town previously known mainly for brewing a good light beer. In Olympia Paul Ingram, a sheriff's deputy, a born-again Christian, and an active member of his county's Republican committee, assumed the role of local monster fallen from virtue. He eventually admitted to sexually abusing his children and conducting Satanic rites in the woods on the outskirts of town. As Frederick Crews summarizes matters, Ingram was "thought to have raped both of his daughters as well as one of his sons innumerable times, to have passed the daughters around sexually as poker nights at home turned into gang rapes, to have hideously tortured the girls and forced them and his wife to have sex with goats and dogs, and to have murdered and cannibalized many babies at huge gatherings of his Satanic cult—where, be it noted, long gowns, pitchforks, and 'Viking hats' were *de rigueur*."[28] Though the authorities dug and dug in the woods, no bodies of the supposedly sacrificed children ever materialized. No evidence, beyond Ingram's testimony, ever confirmed the dark accusations. Shortly before Ingram's daughters recovered their memories of abuse and got the ball rolling, the family sat companionably down together to watch Geraldo Rivera's prime-time special, *Devil Worship: Exposing Satan's Underground*.

Ingram showed an extraordinary ability to "recover" repressed memories of his supposed crimes. When Ofshe, who is well-versed in the psychodynamics of satanic possession, visited Olympia, he was able to plant memories in Ingram with little difficulty. Ofshe told the sheriff's deputy that his daughter and son had recalled his forcing them to have sex together in front of him—something that neither ever claimed. Before long, Paul Ingram was manufacturing memories that worked in perfect corroboration. He had somehow comprehended his role as latter-day Gothic villain, and he played the script out just as dutifully as he had served as sheriff's deputy and Republican stalwart.

In the Olympia case, an epidemic of recovered memories, of internalized Gothic, burst into the public domain and created a Gothic scenario comparable to the Salem witch scare. The fact that in the entire town of Olympia no one had the combination of authority and sanity needed to effectively tell everybody concerned to calm down and go home suggests more than a little about the Gothic dimension of premillennial American life. Saturated with Gothic fictions from all sides, the residents of Olympia found it plausible enough that an outrageous Gothic melodrama would actually unfold among them. Ingram received a twenty-year prison term.

Academic intellectuals, for their part, have begun to develop an interest in pop culture and so, inevitably, in Gothic. With the advent of what's come to be called cultural studies, media renderings of the Bobbitt case are stuff to be analyzed, as is the persona of Michael Jackson, and the many books about the O. J. Simpson trial. These phenomena tend to be approached with some skepticism, as emanations of a deceptive consumer culture. Intellectuals want to pause and check the ingredients in the delights on offer in contemporary Wonderland.

But the terms of contemporary intellectual analysis are themselves worth some scrutinizing. For the fin-de-siècle academic world has a Gothic mode of its own. Much, though surely not all, of what is called theory draws on Gothic idioms. Its subject is haunting. In the language of theory the virtuous villain, the monster of morality, gets renamed. Like the Gothic novelists, academic theoreticians often presume to identify the brutal and coercive, but apparently civilizing, good. In Freudian thinking, I suggested, the virtuous sadist takes the name of the superego. Since *Civilization and Its Discontents,* some of the most talented intellectuals in the West have been at pains to rename and recharacterize Freud's masterpiece of Gothic invention, the over-I.

Jacques Derrida's antagonist is the metaphysics of presence, the phantom-form of truth that haunts Western culture. Though strain as one will to exorcise the text of Western philosophy, metaphysics, like the relentless poltergeist it is, always reappears elsewhere, sometimes in the body of one's own writing. Thus the work of deconstruction, like the work of psychoanalysis strictly conceived, is never-ending. Haunting is interminable. The Freudian-Marxist members of the Frankfurt School denounce the hubris of Enlightenment, in which reason banishes all emotion, myth, and tradition. Feminists assault the omnipotent patriarch in the front office and in the psyche.

Slavoj Žižek, of the former Yugoslavia, finds his Gothic antagonist in the Father of Enjoyment, a rapacious, cruel id that enjoins endless consumption (he's capitalism's huckster), though without satisfaction, and does so in the voice of the authoritative superego. Buy or die! Žižek speaks once in fact of "the obscene and revengeful figure of the Father-of-Enjoyment, of this figure split between cruel revenge and crazy laughter, as, for example, the famous Freddie [sic] from *Nightmare on Elm Street*."[29]

But the most intriguing exponent of Gothic theory is surely Michel Foucault, who is also, arguably, the 1990s' most influential thinker for both the social sciences and the humanities. His haunting agency, which is everywhere and nowhere, as evanescent and insistent as a resourceful spook, is called Power. Power enforces circumscribed identities on us and compels us to work at maximum intensity, squeezing out every productive juice. But it does so not through confrontation, not through denial and coercion, but through perpetual surveillance. Power works by exploiting the many institutional means at society's disposal to observe and evaluate individuals. Working through the mechanisms of ongoing scrutiny and analysis, Power generates sets of terms, vocabularies, that lock us all into inert roles. They lock us in because they are institutionally enforced. The student *is* her grades, and transcript, and psychological profile. Power's terms are also the most ready—for some of us they are the exclusive—means through which we can represent ourselves to ourselves.

Then there is also the pleasure of wielding the terms, wielding Power (or at least imagining that one is doing so). For as well as being observed, we are also, as more responsibility devolves upon us, likely to be doing more and more of Power's scrutinizing, codifying work. We are all, in any event, the circuitry through which the currents of Power pass. Power, Foucault says, "needs to be considered as a productive network which runs through the whole social body, much more than as a negative instance whose function is repression."

Power "circulate[s] in a manner at once continuous, uninterrupted, adapted, and 'individualized.'"[30]

Unlike the bourgeoisie, whom Marx cast as the oppressive civilizing force, Power does not exist in a determinate space. It doesn't have tangible presence. And thus one cannot confront Power; one can only encounter its temporary and generally unwitting agents, even as one is probably functioning as such an agent in some other context oneself. Power, it's clear enough to see, has capacities of motion and transformation that make it a *preternatural* force. It's something more potent than mere humanity. And it possesses us, haunts us.

Can we triumph over Foucault's Gothic spirit of oppression? Hardly. We can't even find it to effect a confrontation. Though it can find us. Like the Fog, in John Carpenter's horror movie of that name, Power is a complex of nefarious energies that seeps into and through our lives, penetrating society and individuals on a molecular level, and from which escape is impossible. Under such a domain, real change is not tenable. Any resistance would be absorbed by the discourses of Power, lost in the Fog.

The forces of nefarious authority that theory identifies are understood to haunt culture at every level. To deconstruct metaphysics, in Derrida's fashion, is to exorcise the ghosts of patriarchal power, the fathers with their coercive truth. So too, theoretical feminism avers, must we cleanse the psyche of old patriarchal ghosts.

What disturbs me about these imperatives, which seem in many ways admirable, is their implication that the antagonist has a supernatural vitality and resourcefulness that makes it virtually impossible to defeat. What ought to be a political and cultural analysis set in sharply secular terms, becomes, through its appropriation of—or by—a Gothic idiom, a story about ghosts and the supernatural. In each case, an analytic method that might have as its objective a critique of Gothic culture, with all of its facile pessimism, un-self-consciously reproduces Gothic assumptions.

In these sections on the three forms of fin-de-siècle Gothic—terror, apocalyptic, and internalized—I have been considering the ways that Gothic conventions have crossed over into purportedly nonfiction realms. But it might pay to turn back to our beginnings and to look again, now with a slightly more experienced eye, at a few of the avowedly fictional forms of '90s Gothic entertainment.

Consider Anne Rice's stylish vampires. Part of what makes books like *Interview with the Vampire* popular, I suspect, is that they depart so strikingly and, for our moment, aptly from the tradition of vampire literature. Up until recently, one was expected to be fascinated with vampires, to be mesmerized by their glamour, their weird allure. But finally one sided with the middle-class characters who pulled themselves together, realized that, yes, the old legends were indeed true, then contrived to drive the stake into Dracula's heart, or trap him out of doors so he'd dissolve into dust at sunrise. The traditional vampire tales played out the theme of modern revolution. The overthrow and death of the aristocracy was dramatized once more. The village blacksmith is eligible to become a werewolf only; to be one of the undead some nobility of blood—or exquisite, aristocratic beauty—is generally required.

Rice reversed the scenario. She seems to have sensed the fact that in the age of the Reagan-Bush plutocracy, readers would be more than happy to throw their allegiances to the higher orders. So in the tale of Louis and Lestat one is invited to identify with the victimizers, the master race of vampires, against the pale, quivering mortals. The vampires are cultivated, worldly, European, sophisticated (at least as a very smart rube would construe sophistication). The victims are pathetic. They aren't very good at fighting back. Maybe they don't deserve to live.

Stephen King, who is often lumped together with Rice, is a very different kind of writer. King loves kids. (Rice features a displaced pedophilia—rapturous blood-sucking between kids and grown-ups, rather than straight-up sex—as one of the attractions of *Interview with the Vampire*.) King's favorite children, usually boys, are always finding themselves in the midst of corrupt, degraded adult societies. The evil that kicks in—a shape-shifting clown in *It,* vampires in *Salem's Lot,* hotel-haunting demons in *The Shining*—tends to be a manifestation of the rotten world the grown-ups have made and are trying to hand on to their children. The adults in King novels are often adulterous, alcoholic, mean, greedy, bigoted, and above all blind to the horrors unfolding around them. The kids, and especially the central kid, see things as they really are. On the subject of childhood, King is rather Wordsworthian.

But unlike Wordsworth, who can meditate impressively on childhood's end ("the years that bring the philosophic mind"), King can't seem to conceive any image of adulthood that's not soaked in worldly corruption. Unless, that is, you grow up—as we're often led to understand that the good kid, the bookish, decent, perceptive one, will—into a prolific, hyper-imaginative, but still humane and down-to-earth author of popular books (250 million in print). Who can disagree with King when he protests against racism, anti-Semitism, homophobia? His heart's in the right place. But he merely invites his readers to relive their childhoods with him, to take a self-righteous vacation away from their day-to-day immersion in the adult world. He's got nothing much to send them back to that world with, or nothing much that would be likely to help change it.

King comes off as a moralist, a liberal, and something of a 1960s plaid-shirt-type good guy. Unlike Poe, who thinks that humans are mostly damned and doomed from the start, Rousseauian King sees evil as something that gets added on, a product of socialization into a bad world. Rice, much more of our moment, asks us to find predatory evil sexy and the height of all sophistication. She helps us learn to sneer at victims. King can be mildly edifying; Rice's *Interview*—to adapt a line of Hunter Thompson's—is the sort of thing that the whole hep world would be reading if the Nazis had won the war.

Gothic energies are also alive in fin-de-siècle movies and books that don't present themselves as overt horror fare. Take the seeming-sweet Disney contraption *The Lion King*. *Lion King* features scrawny, wily Scar as its villain. Scar is—as any psychoanalyst or experienced reader of Gothic fiction would tell you—the nasty double of the good father, King Mufasa. Scar comes to the fore when little Simba, the hero, begins flexing his muscles. "I just can't wait to be king," the Oedipal runt chants, even while Mufasa is alive and in his prime. Mufasa perishes, killed by his dark brother Scar and—the analyst might add—his son's murderous wishes.

Scar's voice, courtesy of Jeremy Irons, is that of a cultivated, world-weary, gay man. He sounds like Gore Vidal with a significant hangover. And Scar (whose name as much as says trauma) has designs on little Simba. Simba: "You're so weird"; Scar (with purring innuendo): "You have no idea." As they're beginning to bond, Scar issues Simba the molesters' mantra: "Remember, it's our little secret."[31] The movie taps into and elaborates children's hostile fantasies against their parents, and their remorse about those fantasies as well. It also provokes and exploits fear of predatory adults. How many times will children need to see Scar overthrown before they've unburdened themselves of accumulated guilt and fright?

While young children watch *The Lion King* and learn to read with kid fright books from R. L. Stine's Goosebumps series, their older brothers and sisters relax with his Fear Street volumes, probably the most popular preteen books in America. Or they catch a music video featuring Madonna, alternately Gothic victim and villain, masochist in a dungeon collar, sadist flourishing her whip. (Gothic is one of the most common aesthetics for rock videos.) There is Goth rock proper and a Goth clothing style as well. Popular computer games, from Myst to Doom, draw copiously on the Gothic idiom. ("It's not all that easy," observes Jason Bell, an executive with Kesmai, a computer game development company, "to think of a highly popular CD game that isn't Gothic.") Late adolescents, who aspire to sophisticatedly decadent pleasures, can savor the S & M depictions of photographer Robert Mapplethorpe. (My favorite finds RM in full demonic self-portraiture, with trainee horns on his head and bullwhip-tail trailing sadly from his bum.)

The current reader who wants to aim higher than Stephen King may engage with one of our profound Gothicists, Toni Morrison (about whom I'll have more to say later) or Don DeLillo, though there are hordes of serious writers who have lately been making use of the Gothic idiom. A brief list: William Gaddis, Jeanette Winterson, John Hawkes, Thomas Pynchon, William Burroughs, Joyce Carol Oates, Norman Mailer, Robert Coover, Angela Carter, Patrick McGrath, Thomas Disch, Kathy Acker.

But Gothic fiction, highbrow or low, pales when it enters competition with renderings of worldly events: the stream of Gothic horrors we find in the news stories, featuring a line of fin-de-siècle Othello/Iagos. Why bother producing a film like *Priests* or writing a novel like Tom Disch's *The Priest: A Gothic Romance,* when there are better stories, and purportedly true ones, on TV and in national magazines? Why bother with

Hannibal Lecter when we have figures like Jeffrey MacDonald, who murdered his entire family and blamed it on a Manson-type cult that chanted "Acid is groovy/Kill the pigs" while carrying out the deed?

Having now mapped the 1990s Gothic domain, we are in a position to pose some questions. What is the function of current true-life Gothic? What cultural work does it do? How does it read and change its audience? Why do we seem to need it now, at the edge of the millennium? To answer these questions, it may be illuminating to turn back in the direction of past Gothic productions and to see what a powerful force Gothic has been, how it *can* function socially.

Ann Radcliffe was a timid woman with debilitating asthma and a tepid, overrefined prose style. But she was also one of the great inventors of English literature. She took over the costumery, personae, and props from Walpole's trivial, engrossing *Castle of Otranto* (published in the year she was born, 1764) and began to charge them with the anxieties of her age.

Radcliffe's grand hero-villain Montoni is an aristocrat, an Italian, and a Catholic, and so, at least in the minds of an English audience, capable of anything. (Since Shakespeare and Marlowe, the English haven't been inclined to dissociate Italy and Machiavelli.) Radcliffe describes Montoni as "unprincipled, dauntless, cruel and enterprising." She wants him attractive, but not too attractive. His courage is written off as "a sort of animal ferocity": he is brave because he feels no inhibitions; no fear, but no pity either.[32] The goodness of Radcliffe's characters is measured by their ability to respond to landscapes beautiful and sublime, and Montoni is numb to the gorgeous mountains of his birthplace. But of course, Montoni is also handsome, wickedly so. He is, in short, the archetypal unenlightened aristocrat; both magnetic and appalling, he focuses

English ambivalence about the old, noble orders that may be passing away.

Emily St. Aubert, the heroine of *Mysteries of Udolpho,* is a prototype for the hordes of Gothic heroines who have since found themselves running wildly down long dark corridors, sheer white nightgowns billowing out and gleaming in the moonlight. (In the latter-day political-Gothic film, *The Pelican Brief,* you find Darby Shaw/Julia Roberts, Emily's descendant, flying at full speed through underground parking garages and hotel hallways—where's my car? where's my room? who am I?—the stuff of current-day anxiety dreams.) Emily runs in fear; Emily faints. After almost every stern tongue-lashing from Montoni, and she gets plenty, Emily goes back to her room and soaks the pillow with tears.

But though Emily may scurry, faint, and weep, she also periodically draws herself together and stands up to Montoni. Her mind, we are given to understand, is at least as keen as his, and her virtue gives added point to her reason. Emily is a young woman of Sensibility, the eighteenth-century prototype for the Romantic imagination. The faith in feeling as a universally available means for apprehending the truth was central to the belief in general equality that fired political change throughout Europe in the revolutionary period. In the court of the sympathetic reader's mind, reasonable and passionate Emily, and the middle-class ethos she embodies, win every exchange.

Jane Austen parodies Mrs. Radcliffe's heroines sharply enough in *Northanger Abbey,* but Austen's own freedom to create figures like the independent Elizabeth Bennet in *Pride and Prejudice* evolved in part from Radcliffe's putting female consciousness at the center of a major work. As the literary historian Marilyn Butler observes, "While not supporting nor presumably consciously sharing the feminist ideological position, Ann Radcliffe pushes further than anyone yet the novel's technique for seeing the world through explicitly female eyes."[33]

Matthew Gregory Lewis was, in person, mild enough, a bug-eyed, halting little man who became London's literary lion in 1796. *The Monk* shocked everyone, its author included, who seems to have been puzzled about the reasons for his book's success and about what it was that so troubled his moralizing critics. In any event, Lewis spent the rest of his life trying to make up for his literary sin: he wrote better-mannered books; he went to the West Indies to introduce tenderhearted means for managing his plantations' slaves.

Monk Lewis composed his first novel with his mother in mind: she needed the money. He dashed the book off in just a few months and then became the most popular scandal in town, the Norman Mailer of the year. He developed friendships with Shelley and Byron (whom he bored half to death). All of the so-called Romantics read him. Wordsworth hated his work bitterly, associating it with the kind of excessive stimulation required by people who had been numbed into a stupor by city life.

The virtuous villain of *The Monk* is Ambrosio, whose pulpit eloquence mesmerizes all of Madrid. People flock from everywhere to hear him. He's handsome, inspired, brilliant, but his own perfection hardens his heart to the weaknesses of others and eventually makes him more susceptible to temptation. (In *Civilization and Its Discontents* Freud, who detests religion, grins over the anchorites who forever have tempting demons buzzing around their heads: they force too much renunciation on themselves, outraging their instincts, which then come back with redoubled force.) Matilda, the book's female lead, and a character just as engrossing as Ambrosio, gets access to the monastery by disguising herself as a young boy. She then succeeds in seducing Ambrosio. It's not hard, since Ambrosio is already aroused by a portrait of the virgin that Matilda has

posed for. But soon he wearies of Matilda and seeks an innocent, like his former self, to corrupt.

He finds Antonia, a fifteen-year-old girl. With the help of
Satan, called up by Matilda, Ambrosio gets into Antonia's
bedroom and assaults her, but is stopped by Elvira, Antonia's
mother, whom he kills. He gives Antonia a sleeping potion
and has her pronounced dead and consigned to the catacombs
below a convent; there, surrounded by the dead, he rapes,
then murders her. The soldiers of the Inquisition capture
Ambrosio, but he escapes from them by selling his soul to
the Devil. (The adolescent sensibility regnant in the book
ought to be, by now, perceptible enough.) He's then trans-
ported by demons to a mountaintop, where he is tortured to
death ("the eagles of the rock tore his flesh piecemeal") after
being informed that Elvira was his mother and Antonia his
sister.[34]

Matters get yet kinkier: Matilda is revealed to have been a
demon attendant on Satan, a male who masqueraded as a female pretending to be a boy. Ambrosio is a superego-ridden
neurotic. Like Norman Bates in *Psycho*, he comes to detest
what turns him on: he kills Antonia; he suffers Matilda only
because he fears her. Simultaneously virtuous and base, Ambrosio embodies the divided self found in—or imposed
upon—so many of our fin-de-siècle objects of cultural fascination.

Ambrosio and Montoni represent the twin objects of revolutionary hatred, the priest and the nobleman. Yet they are
neither French (and thus directly associable with the events
surrounding the Revolution) nor English. The late-eighteenth-century British reader could generalize the critique of
authority in *The Monk* and *Udolpho* as far as he or she might
wish. To some, the books were no doubt about faraway problems; to others, they spoke about English abuses and about the
need for revolution at home.

In the year that Radcliffe published *Udolpho*, William Blake brought out "London," a poem that spoke out against depravities of church and state:

> How the Chimney-sweeper's cry
> Every black'ning Church appalls;
> And the hapless Soldier's sigh,
> Runs in blood down Palace walls.[35]

The poor chimney sweep and the forgotten soldier cry out, but palace and church, aristocracy and priesthood are deaf. There's little doubt as to how Blake (a reader of Mrs. Radcliffe and other Gothic writers) would be disposed to use books like *The Monk* and *Udolpho:* to elaborate his protests against the authoritarian god Urizen and his earthly retainers.

Nor are the political and ethical energies of Gothic necessarily spent; time hasn't wasted the idiom's power. To show as much, I want to offer a couple of instances of effective contemporary Gothic—Gothic that does some useful cultural work. My first example is rather slight—it's generally billed as a children's movie, in fact—but my second example, Wes Craven's *Nightmare on Elm Street,* seems to me a work of lowbrow genius.

Tim Burton's claymation classic, *The Nightmare before Christmas,* is a Gothic comedy populated by marvelously wrought clay monsters. The conceit of *Nightmare* is that the denizens of Halloween Town—ghosts, ghouls, vampires, and the like, all under the leadership of Hamlet-like Jack, the Pumpkin King—decide to colonize Christmas. Jack *wants* to be a good, genial Santa Claus, but somehow his demonic nature continually rips through. He terrifies the kids by popping severed heads instead of toys from out of his bag. Eventually the army has to shoot his sleigh from the sky.

The movie can be rather witty. When Jack decides to deliver a graveyard-type soliloquy in the noble Dane's mode, he pops his own bleached-white head off, flourishes it at arm's length, and holds forth. The film does have a nasty barb in it, though it's small enough. After Jack spends a day or so in Christmas Town and decides that he wants to take over, he goes off and gets piles of books about the meaning of Christmas. Yet read as he will, he can't figure it out. Jack's puzzlement over what Christmas is really all about doesn't stop his coup. Jack gets Santa kidnapped ("Take Mister Santa Claus, put him in a box / Bury him for ninety years, then see if he talks," sing the three Halloween brats who push Claus into the big bag) and haunts the holiday. But the point is that Christmas is easy enough to haunt, easy to grab, because it has no integral meaning. It's just a bunch of gooey rituals—present-swapping, light-stringing, and candy-eating—that aren't attached to any larger meanings. The holiday's been voided of spiritual content. Once you take over the rituals, you've taken Christmas. The movie, minor as it is, has enough taste to avoid a bald statement of its designs, but the point does get made: something's rotten in the state of Christmas.

Now consider Wes Craven's *Nightmare on Elm Street*. *Nightmare* spawned a number of sequels (none entirely created by Craven until the disastrous *New Nightmare*), and a few of them prospered by submitting Freddy Krueger, the films' Gothic monster, to ridicule. In a coda to one, he engages in a little break-dancing. But in his first film manifestation, Freddy is an arresting figure.

In what is, at least for me, *Nightmare on Elm Street*'s most memorable scene, Freddy encounters Tina, whom he'll soon slash to death with his weapon of choice, a ragged glove equipped with long, elegant blades, like Mandarin fingernails. Freddy's been burned; he has the scarred face of someone caught on the edge of a nuclear blast. He speaks in an intimately mocking bass voice—the voice of conscience gone sadistic—and laughs a hearty, madhouse laugh. When Tina gets her first good look at him, she exclaims, not unexpectedly, "Please, God!" "This," Freddy responds, flourishing the claw, "is God!"

Soon, with a swipe Freddy severs two fingers of his opposite hand, sending them flying through the air while a bilious-looking liquid squirts from the stumps. As the fingers sail, Freddy grins, deeply self-satisfied.

In Melville's *Moby Dick* there's a scene where sharks attack a whale carcass. The harpooners come on to rescue the valuable whale and spear some of the attacking fish in the tails. The sharks are already feeding wildly, but when they're cut they go mad and start striking their own exposed bowels. Freddy is something akin to those sharks. The self-amputating slash is the trademark of a creature so ferocious that there's nothing it won't do. But the grin indicates that there's a bizarre intelligence at work, a refined capacity to sense what a given victim is going to find most horrifying.

Freddy comes from the other end of the social order from Montoni and Ambrosio; he's a dingy bum dressed in a broken fedora and football hooligan's cast-off sweater. In the mid-1980s, when *Nightmare* came out, a collaborative effort between the far left and the right had filled the streets with homeless, miserable men and women. While Reagan lowered and lowered the so-called economic safety net, a generation of left-wing therapists and public health officials, many of them influenced by R. D. Laing and Michel Foucault, had decided that there was more than method, there was potential illumination in madness, and that not to let the disturbed roam free was oppression. So the streets of every city, but most sensationally New York, were filled with men and women in psychic distress. And over time such people often developed personalities that brought the prophet-speaker's of Blake's *London* a few notches up. Lock eyes with the wrong person on Lower Broadway, and you might find yourself featured in a narrative that also included the cast from the Book of Revelation. Freddy, the bum, draws on fear of that underclass, a fear that persists. Suppose one of them decided to take revenge, to take up residence in your studio, your cellar, your psyche?

Freddy's domain is the boiler room, the place where the school pervert, be he janitor or teacher, goes to ply his vice. And Craven knows how to make of the boiler room a genuinely terrible place. It is mazelike, factorylike, full of the hissing and steaming of ongoing inscrutable production. What's being produced? Here Craven has a striking answer, visually conveyed. What is being produced in and through Freddy's boiler rooms—Blake would have called them dark Satanic mills—are people.

Architecture is central to the social polemic of the best terror writing and filmmaking. For a novel or a movie to be in the true terror mode, there must be a horrifying place. The first horrible place, and the one that lives on, through Radcliffe's castle, Lewis's monastery, and Freddy's boiler room, is the Bastille. The Bastille was the building that came to symbolize all of the oppression against which the French people waged their revolution. The Bastille represented the monarchy's power to grab up people arbitrarily and close their lives down, submit them to misery and silence, disappear them. Throughout the French Revolution, the haunted prison was the sign of cruel and unusual rulership.

Montoni haunts the castle; Ambrosio, the monastery of the Capuchins, and especially the catacombs beneath. These figure church and state, the forces that weigh too hard upon society, that need renovation. Craven is, if possible, even more preoccupied with institutions than his predecessors in terror. *Nightmare* conducts a tour of every consequential institution in Elmstreetville. The home is the first and most dramatically maligned establishment, but the film also presents scenes of school, the police department, a clinic, and a church.

About two-thirds of the way through the movie there is an image that clinches matters. Freddy comes after the children in their dreams, slashes them there so they die in real life. He's a haunting figure, a figure of the psyche. How to defend against him? When Nancy's mother sees that her daughter is in danger she takes good, pragmatic steps. She calls the serviceman. In a full frontal shot we see the result of his work: a square, squat bourgeois home with bars fixed to all the windows, as though the specter were trying to break in, as though Freddy came from outside. And it's the bars on the window that will impede Nancy's escape from inside the house, when she manages to coax Freddy out of the dream-world.

The function of eighteenth-century terror-Gothic, suggests Leslie Fiedler, was "to shock the bourgeoisie into an awareness of what a chamber of horrors its own smugly regarded world really was."[36] Walk down into the basement of Nancy's house and you find Freddy's boiler room. Walk a flight down from the first floor at school and you're there, too. On the way to the boiler room a hall monitor, who speaks in Freddy's voice and waves his claw, accosts Nancy. Freddy fits in fine with the system. Up above, while Freddy chases his prey through the steaming labyrinth, the students, who are nearly sleeping in their chairs, listen to the teacher drone on about how, in Shakespeare's tragedies, what is apparent isn't what's real, how you have to penetrate below the surface. Below their particular surface—unknown to all but Nancy—is the boiler room.

Craven's joke, if you can call it that, is that in the world of *Nightmare* everybody is asleep when they are supposed to be awake. It's only when you fall asleep that you see life for what it is. Which is what? Which is the domination of Freddy, the child killer. To see Freddy in one's dreams is to encounter a compressed and hysterical but, the film avers, accurate image for the waking world. Freddy wants to do to you, if you're an adolescent, quickly and agonizingly what the institutional world wants to do to you slowly, painlessly, numbingly—put you to sleep, inure you to a death in life.

Freddy has access to the prison; Freddy has free rein at the fancy clinic where Nancy goes for treatment; Freddy doesn't make the funeral when a macho character (Rod, naturally) is buried, but Craven does make a point of having the minister tie himself quickly in knots: in one breath he observes that he who lives by the sword shall die by it, and that we ought to judge not lest we be judged.

A film like *Nightmare* is generally judged by parents to be a waste of time, a vacuous thrill-show. But if I am right the film is ferocious in its indictment of the society that parents are leaving to their children. It's a society in which, despite tranquil appearances, Freddy rules. Virtually all of the adults in the film are mean and self-seeking, most dramatically Nancy's parents. They're all Freddy's stand-ins.

Craven is making an adolescent movie; he's protesting against certain conditions found in schools and clinics and police stations—the sorts of places Michel Foucault liked to write disparaging anatomies of—on behalf of kids. But this is not an unprecedented position: it was Dickens's and Blake's. It was Twain's in *Huckleberry Finn*. These writers suggested that a society was to be judged centrally by how it treated its children. Part of what distinguishes Craven's protest is that it does not stop with a negative reaction to unbearable forces. It also offers a possible way out, which I'll describe later. For now, I want to return to the American 1990s.

What about our own culture of Gothic? Does it register the sorts of protest, muted or grand, that one finds in the likes of

Radcliffe, Lewis, and Craven? Does it use its sometimes out-rageous hyperbole to cut through the crust of convention and make us see the world afresh?

Consider, for a moment, a commonplace current produc-tion that often employs the Gothic plot. The afternoon talk show is something of a hybrid between internalized and ter-ror Gothic. One might say that the genius of the talk show is that it has the immediacy of fiction or film—they're all so intimate, these stories of suffering and abuse—and the pres-tige of fact. Consider the victimizers, who make such regular appearances on the shows. This is the husband or son who has persecuted the family. He has done unspeakable things. He sits hangdog under the hot lights, wagging his head in doleful assent as his victims recite the litany of his crimes. And—in true modern Gothic fashion—it is not only the harm done by the event itself that matters, there is also the fact that the trauma continues to despoil the lives of the vic-tims. Its memory eats away from within, a cancer of the psy-che.

But then it's the perpetrator's turn, and something odd hap-pens. Generally the victimizer is himself haunted/ad-dicted/obsessed. He is addicted to drinking, to drugs, to sex, to abuse. (Oprah calls herself a food addict.) He confesses and then disavows responsibility. As the novelist Charles Baxter puts it: "Afternoon talk shows have only apparent antagonists. Their sparring partners are not real antagonists because the bad guys usually confess then immediately disavow . . . The story is trying to find a source of meaning, but in the story, everyone is disclaiming responsibility. Things have just hap-pened."[37] Everyone acts as though he or she were, in some fashion, possessed, including the villain.

Himself haunted, the victimizer haunts others, making them dependent on him for something to fight back against or some-one to rescue. They become addicted to the pain and emotional expression he provokes, become addicted to catharsis. The victimizer functions as a source of meaning. All of one's unhappiness, discontent, and grief can be traced back to a simple source. One is delivered from the burden of telling a complex story about oneself, a story that might entail reflections on economic injustice and sexism, or one's own selfishness, indolence, or brutality. The story is personal, local, specific, and without moral nuance: everyone disavows; all are as innocent as they are guilty. We might call the phenomenon No-Fault Gothic.

A recent *New Yorker* story about priests and pedophilia ended in a relevantly instructive way. The author described scenes of sexual malfeasance on the part of God's anointed that would, I suspect, have given Monk Lewis pause:

> One priest who had a young boy routinely perform oral sex on him would give him absolution from the sin while the boy was still on his knees. Another priest told a boy while fondling him that what he did was "an expression of God's love" and that "God is blessing this act." A third priest told his young victims, "I am God's instrument and God wants you to have pleasure right now, in this way." A woman has charged that as a girl she told Father James Porter in the confessional that a boy had touched her immodestly; Porter is alleged to have insisted on a demonstration and to have taken the girl into his section of the confessional and fondled her. Priests have admitted to scanning the congregation for child sex objects while saying Mass and ejaculating while at the altar.[38]

The author, Paul Wilkes, gives no quarter in describing the priests' acts, providing a level of ethical commentary far beyond Oprah Winfrey's habitual range. We're not dealing here with No-Fault Gothic, per se.

But Wilkes does close the piece in a rather disturbing way. He ends by saying that if the Church is to regain its standing, it must "confess its own sins and do something about them."[39] That is, a church solution is offered to solve the church's difficulties. Confession, one of the seven sacraments, administered by priests, becomes the metaphor of choice for Catholic renewal. There is no hint of the more comprehensive—and socially oriented—view that the entire authoritarian system of Catholicism, based in part on the systematic inculcation of sexual guilt (through agencies like confession), might have something to do with the problem. Overly rigid prohibitions and taboos can invite transgression. One might have said—as the young Monk Lewis surely would have—that the ban on priestly sex, combined with the church's narrow attitudes toward sex in general, could be in some measure responsible for priests' indulgence in pedophilia.

Yet if current Gothic is often no-fault or, even in its more sophisticated manifestations, too narrow in its range of explanation, too programmatically, self-servingly apolitical, it can also be rather frightening. Because what's recounted on talk shows and written up in the news could also happen to you. You could be—perhaps somewhere in the repressed past you have been—a victim of comparable abuse. Watch out. At the same time, because the victimizer is himself possessed, haunted, a similar addiction could take you over. It's the Gothic wisdom: we all lead a double life; and our other, our *it*, could choose any moment to reassert itself. Thus the films about a character who's sweet normality itself on the outside, but harbors a demon within: *The Hand that Rocks the Cradle*, *Wolf*, *Fatal Attraction*, *Single White Female*. Be afraid, very afraid, and of nothing so much as yourself.

Commentators tell us that the O. J. Simpson case exposed bitter divisions between blacks and whites in fin-de-siècle America and that learning that those divisions exist is of some cultural value. But it seems to me that the rendering of the case didn't *expose* racial divisions: everyone knew about those. Rather, the major media's Gothic rendering of the case served to *deepen* race hatred in America. At the center of that rendering was the Gothic fiction of the split personality, the Jekyll and Hyde motif, which was adapted in the ugliest possible way. Simpson, suggested *Time*, *Newsweek*, and many other sources, was black inside, white outside. And how many other black men, we were invited to ask, are of the same ilk?

It's not surprising that much of black America collaborated on a Gothic novel about the case that was of a dramatically different sort. In that version, O. J. Simpson was not the hero-villain, he was the victim. The hero-villains were the members of the Los Angeles Police Department who had, it was thought, framed Simpson, an innocent black man. In concocting this Gothic scenario, Simpson's defense team, led by Johnnie Cochran and Robert Shapiro, played a major role. The defense story argued that, as Jeffrey Toobin puts it, "Simpson was the victim of a wide-ranging conspiracy of racist law enforcement officials who had fabricated and planted evidence in order to frame him for a crime he did not commit."[40] This story was almost certainly fictitious; surely no hard evidence arose to confirm it.

But the defense was playing to an experience shared by black Los Angeleans, and black Americans overall, that was not at all fictitious: the experience of oppression by white law enforcement officials. In this scenario, society had, in the phrase of the critic John Bayley, become a Gothic institution. The L.A. Police Department, and its supporting agencies, looked to those who endorsed this Gothic plot something like what home and school and clinic—and police department—look like to Wes Craven in *A Nightmare on Elm Street*.

Both of the Gothic novels that America wrote during the Simpson case were exciting, dramatic, powerful. But in their fully developed forms—that blacks harbor a second, demonic self inside; that whites and their institutions are racist to the core—both fictions breed paranoia and hate. Neither story is true; neither will bring us closer to racial reconciliation. (Those commentators who said that the Simpson case helpfully exposed racial animosities were often implicitly defending their well-rewarded and incendiary Gothic renderings of the case.) Without a cultural appetite for debased Gothic, without the currency of Gothic forms, without the sensationalistic impulses that went into the nation's two Gothic versions of the case, we would have had to arrive at more patient and humane ways of describing a horrible event. Understanding and detached judgment might have replaced paranoic flights, and in the wake of the case, we might be a calmer, more confident nation than we are. "Mythic humanity," says Walter Benjamin, "pays with fear for intercourse with daemonic forces."

Similarly, rants about AIDS and environmental disaster, framed in the apocalyptic Gothic mode, spawn guilt and fear but contribute nothing to progress. The many cases of recovered memory have created riveting news stories, but little serious inquiry into what actually drives young people to their accusations. Almost no one has proposed using the publicized cases of priestly child abuse as a basis for church reform. Damage control has been the order of the day. The unfortunate guests on talk shows may make the audience glad to be the relatively normal sorts they are, but it's highly unlikely that the shows expand anyone's breadth of tolerance much more than does the carnival freak show. If eighteenth-century Gothic helped its readers break through convention and see the world freshly, our Gothic, at least in the majority of its popular forms, seems to do anything but that. Current pop Gothic breeds fear and anger, shuts down the power to make humane distinctions, eclipses thought.

But I've been talking about tabloid Gothic. What about the sophisticated brands? What about, say, academic theory? In his great book, *Discipline and Punish*, Michel Foucault brilliantly delineates the transformation of royal power, which emanates from the king, into the intricate web of insinuating, observing power that haunts us today. With great subtlety he shows how the power that simply repressed, simply said no, has been displaced by networks of power in which all observers, with the aid of complicated observation technologies, are perpetually observed: a world of nonphysical, silent coercion. It is the world emblematized by the haunted all-seeing Gothic tower at the center of Foucault's vision, the panopticon.

And what are we to do about it? In a famous remark, Foucault observed that to engage in Utopian thinking is to contribute something to current oppression. This is true, presumably, because discourse is power: when we speak through the authoritative institutional channels, especially in hopeful terms, we affirm those institutions, those channels: we endorse things as they are. There's no way out.

One of our most formidable novelists, Don DeLillo, develops a vision of power much like Foucault's, one in which you can locate no fixed force of coercion to oppose, and ends up with what I at least take to be a tired image of hope, the writer as truth-telling, Hemingwayesque outsider. DeLillo, at least, has an answer, though it is conventional enough; Foucault gives nothing. No-hope Gothic. Dead-end Gothic.

Dead-end, no-fault, paranoic: our current Gothic modes invite us to be afraid, but not, in general, to fight back. They suggest that we're our own worst enemy and propose no cogent defense. They counsel us to despair about political change and social reform. They offer us only the satisfaction that can come from complete fatalism, from giving up.

The Gothic, from its origins, is a reductive mode; its objective is to awaken its audience from dogmatic slumber through hyperbole and melodrama. In the hands of Mary Shelley, Monk Lewis, Ann Radcliffe, and Wes Craven, Gothic reduction becomes a way to intensify experience. But we now find ourselves in a culture where the Gothic idiom has slipped over from fiction and begun to shape and regulate our perception of reality, thrusting us into a world in which crazy militiamen, deranged priests, panoptic power, bizarre molesters, Freddy, Jason, and Leatherface constitute reality. They are—to more and more of us—what's out there. Seeking clarity with too much persistence, we have created a world of brightly toned, lethal cartoons.

But why should the Gothic mode be reaching a point of intensity in the 1990s? Why do we need it now? I might begin to answer this question by drawing an analogy between the first flourishing of Gothic and the one that we now witness. Late-eighteenth-century Gothic was the literature of revolution. From the perspective of Fiedler, revolutionary literature tended in two apparently opposed directions. The Gothic writers were, in the main, progressives. Monk Lewis was, give or take, a man of enlightened political views. He disliked absolutism and superstition, an unresponsive state, and an unbending church.

But the Gothic writers also greatly feared the upshot of their iconoclasm. They feared the freedom they ardently desired, lest it result in chaos or isolation. Thus Fiedler, writing at his hyperbolical best: "The guilt which underlies the gothic and motivates its plots is the guilt of the revolutionary haunted by the (paternal) past which he has been striving to destroy; and the fear that possesses the gothic and motivates its tone is the fear that in destroying the old ego-ideals of Church and State, the West has opened a way for the inruption of darkness: for insanity and the disintegration of the self. Through the pages of the gothic romance, the soul of Europe flees its own darker impulses."[41]

Can we say that our own Gothic mode might also be, in some fashion, a revolutionary cultural form, and that it might betray some of the same fundamental ambivalence that Fiedler shrewdly describes? Yes and no. Our Gothic modes do have a certain sort of revolutionary provenance, but they lack the enriching ambivalence that Fielder ascribes to the eighteenth-century versions.

A fittingly perceptive cultural history of America during the 1960s has yet to be written. That period, so rich in events and personalities, has been poorly served by its chroniclers. But in time, no doubt someone will come fully to describe how civil rights, the struggle for women's rights, the gay movement, the youth movement, a sexual rebellion, and a general drive for broad human enfranchisement took off in the period just before and during the Vietnam War. Suddenly, great masses of Americans who had lived subordinate, secondary lives demanded to be recognized as full citizens, as having as much right to liberty and the pursuit of happiness as the upholders of the box-shouldered, male, heterosexual norm. Fin-de-siècle America continues to reel under those demands, which have grown stronger and clearer, but also, alas, often more simple-minded and self-righteous over time.

It is perhaps not entirely accidental that many '90s Gothic scenarios involve members of these newly insurgent groups in central roles. Our Gothic melodramas teem with transgressor blacks like O. J. Simpson and Michael Jackson; with enraged women like Lorena Bobbitt, Tonya Harding, and the purported victims of once-repressed sexual abuse; and with adolescents and even children in one state or another of sexual abandon. What did this '60s movement to so-called liberation let loose? Has it not, ultimately, led to an age of chaos?

Those are the questions that '90s Gothic modes implicitly pose. For many of our Gothic productions are inspired by a fear that the demons are out of the bottle, never to go back. Fin-de-siècle American Gothic is often motivated by a drive to turn back the clock—to get the uppity women, the blacks, and the young back into their place. (Which is not to say that some of the most avid consumers of '90s Gothic are not women, blacks, and the young.) Like eighteenth-century Gothic, current Gothic displays anxiety over the vast transformations the age has witnessed.

But what our Gothic lacks is the enriching ambivalence of Monk Lewis's mode. Current Gothic productions seem intent on exploiting and stimulating fear. Rarely do we encounter the hope, even tentatively expressed, that many of the transformations born in the 1960s, and still unfolding, may, for all the suffering they've entailed, be for the best. Eighteenth-century Gothic advocated freedom while also indulging fear and nostalgia. Our Gothic is, in the main, nowhere near so richly paradoxical a phenomenon.

One might cite another historical reason for the proliferation of recent Gothic, and that is of course the oncoming millennium. The closing off of a thousand-year period invites apocalyptic thinking, to which current Gothic contributes. The years leading up to 1000 gave rise to countless, elaborate prognostications, many of them dealing with the end of the world. When nothing cataclysmic happened at that first millennium, many believers simply reset their calendars. Some suggested that the current era should not have begun until the year of Christ's death, so that 1033 was the time to beware. Nothing much happened then either.

Premillennial culture is a culture of anxiety. We are overcome with fearful imaginings about the future. One function of Gothic, I've suggested, is to turn free-floating anxiety into suspense. That is, Gothic takes our inchoate fear about what will happen to us and attaches it to a coherent, suspenseful narrative that is due to achieve some resolution. With that resolution anxiety is discharged, at least for a while. Current Gothic, vague but ominous, doesn't offer specific millennial predictions; too many projected days of judgment have come and gone for that. But it does convey a sense of dark foreboding, intimations of some major, and horrible, transformation that will ride in on the year 2000. It turns our pervasive, undirected anxiety into cogent suspense.

At mid-century, many of America's apocalyptic intimations involved the Soviet Union and nuclear holocaust. The lessening of the nuclear threat has, I think, simply dispersed Gothic thinking, made it more various and ingenious. Once there was only one Gothic master-villain in our lives (and something of a hero-villain, too, in that its original promise entailed social justice); with the dwindling of the Soviet Union we need many. From O. J. to the panopticon, we have any number of replacements, each tailored more or less to the race, class, education, and gender of the believer. (For me, you'll recall, no one can beat Richard M. Nixon.)

In the previous pages I have offered a number of motivations for contemporary Gothic, which we might add to the breakup of the USSR, pressures still exerted from the 1960s, and the onset of the millennium. There is also television's technical development from cool to potentially hot medium, which enhances its power to convey violent stimulations, as well as the expansion of channels and the concomitant lowering of an already modest sense of the lowest-common-denominator audience. There is the erosion, abetted by TV, of a shared conception of inviolable private life, such that the horrors of an individual or a family now qualify as common property. We have a right to know the worst about anyone, and immediately. There is the influence of Freud's internalized Gothic image of the psyche, which has penetrated society at every level, often deployed by people who know nothing directly of Freud. There is the current despair with politics, the sense that something is badly wrong with the way we run America, along with a scarcity of plausible programs for change. Like the conservative Edmund Burke's despair over the revolutionary events in France, our own political pessimism has brought forth a rhetoric of Gothic invective. Though unlike Burke, a brilliant political theorist, we often have little more than invective to offer.

Indeed, contemporary Gothic is often an exercise in what we might call the reductive fallacy, the conviction that the worst truth that you can come up with about any person or event is the most consequential truth. The benefit that comes from having the worst-case truth on hand is that you'll never be surprised. You'll never be written off as naive (one of the worst things to be in '90s culture). The downside of Gothic reductionism, though, is timidity, cynicism, fear of life. Like a modern-day Pascal, the neo-Gothicist comes to think that all troubles could be avoided if we would simply stay locked tight in our rooms.

Yet if I were pressed to submit one reason for the contemporary proliferation of Gothic, that reason would in a certain sense be religious. Though most of us Americans claim to believe in God, few of us seem able to believe in God's presence. That is, we do not perceive some powerful force for good shaping the events of day-to-day life in accord with a perceptibly benevolent master plan. Most of us don't have a story that we can believe about the way God's designs are unfolding among us. Whatever God is up to, he is not busying himself unduly with worldly events.

Many of us have, I think, turned from hope in benevolent religion to fascination with the Gothic. There is something to gain in accepting the harsh belief that the world is infested with evil, that all power is corrupt, all humanity debased, and that there is nothing we can do about it. With the turn to contemporary Gothic—no-fault, dead-end, politically impotent though it may be—we recover a horizon of ultimate meaning. We recover something of what is lost with the withdrawal of God from the day-to-day world. With the Gothic, we can tell ourselves that we live in the worst and most barbaric of times, that all is broken never to be mended, that things are bad and fated to be, that significant hope is a sorry joke, the prerogative of suckers. The Gothic, dark as it is, offers epistemological certainty; it allows us to believe that we've found the truth.

Nietzsche saw that when God disappeared from daily life for many in the West during the nineteenth century, the result was . . . the result was precious little; things seemed to go on as before. The change was too vast, too cataclysmic to understand or even to perceive. The news didn't reach us. It was as though the polestar had perished; the light would continue traveling to earth for some time. But now, as the news comes closer, we build up cultural defenses to seal us from the harsh truth that there is no one—no God or gods—but ourselves to take on the burden of creating the human future and of making the world a livable place for all. Gothic despair is a pseudosophisticated way of defending ourselves against the complexity of our problems and the breadth of our responsibilities. It seems that we'd rather have Gothic despair for life's meaning than be compelled to make meanings of our own. We seem frozen, struck with some weird awe, in front of Freddy as he flourishes his blades and croaks, "This is God!"

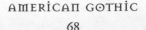

THE WORLD
ACCORDING TO
FORREST GUMP

In their commitment to ultimate despair, 1990s Gothic modes are beholden to the genius of American terror, to Edgar Allan Poe. Poe is our national prophet of death's inevitable victory over life. We know from nearly the beginning that the black cat will return to wreak vengeance; that Fortunato will be walled up in the catacomb where he had hoped to find the cask of amontillado; that the House of Usher will come tumbling down around Roderick. And now it is as though Poe's spirit, like a specter from one of his own tales, has risen up to brood over the fin de siècle.

Poe is in many ways the inheritor of Radcliffe and Lewis; like them he discloses a haunted world. But Poe's Gothic mode is also strikingly different from that of his English predecessors: his is more inward, less socially created, more nightmarish. And Poe's Gothic is without escape.

America is a nation of extremes; we ask more of experience than others and grow more disillusioned and enraged when life does not answer to our hopes. Poe took the already violent modes of revolutionary British Gothic and invested them with an intensity that is altogether American. He is the artist of dead-end Gothic par excellence. The Gothic *forms* that we encounter on *Oprah* and the horror-fest news may belong to Lewis and Radcliffe, to Mary Shelley and to Sigmund Freud, but their dark intensity we owe to the genius of our own land, to Poe.

Harold Bloom observed that "self-reliance, the Emersonian answer to Original Sin, does not exist in the Poe cosmos, where you necessarily start out damned, doomed and dismal." And stay that way, one might add. In Poe—as throughout the 1990s culture of Gothic—the past rises up to devour any attempt to begin anew: the present is fully possessed by long-ago traumas. "No one in a Poe story," Bloom says, "was ever young."[1]

But if Poe is lord, where is Emerson? Where in our culture is the spirit that has competed with Poe for possession of the nation's inner life, the spirit that embodies what many have hoped would be new and singular about the United States? Emerson is our national prophet of self-reliance. He believes that if you trust yourself, speak your truth, do your work with a high heart and a clear mind, then the whole world will eventually come round to you. Your life and thoughts will become a text that others quote all the time, whether they know it or not. So we inevitably quote and reenact Shakespeare and all of our truly great predecessors.

Unlike Poe, whose every story was a burnt offering on its altar, Emerson doesn't believe in Fate, no more than he believes in original sin, or that any man or woman, however lowly, is doomed from the start. Fate is something that we succumb to out of fear; in the Emersonian cosmos fate is an alibi and little more. The only sin, Emerson tells us, is limitation—which means many things, among them that guilt has got to go. Whatever our faults in the past, we need to forget them or redeem them, if in sustaining them we're impeded from doing our work in the present.

And limitation is sin in that Emerson's is a philosophy of ceaseless action. There is little to venerate in our past achievements: "Life only avails, not the having lived." Emerson, at his most spiritually aggressive, preaches perpetual movement: we're most ourselves when we're in the process of transition, going from one project, one identity, one commitment, one metaphor (for Emerson is among other things a philosopher of composition) to the next. Transition doesn't cast out the past (despite the common perception that Emerson doesn't believe in history); rather, transition refigures and renews what's given by culture, politics, and language.

The gap between Emerson's thought and America's European legacy is manifest in his sense of time. True, the past weighs heavily: Emerson says, putting it in a shorthand, "My giant goes with me wherever I go." But Emerson's faith—and here it merges with, or maybe helps create, the highest American faith—is that what is given, however respectable, however onerous, can be changed for the better through the exertions of a confident spirit. Emerson dramatizes a great deal of what would make America different from every past nation: all that is is subject to revision and reform. In Europe, in France in particular, Poe is a figure to reckon with: he inspired Baudelaire, Mallarmé, and Lacan. There is French Freud, there is French Poe, but there never will be French Emerson.

But where is American Emerson now? Where is our counterweight to Poe? Poe's Gothic genius lived on through Hawthorne and Melville and enters the present in a myriad of forms, from Anne Rice's novels to the daytime talk shows of Oprah Winfrey and company. Emerson begot Whitman and Thoreau; Frost; and, in certain regards, Wallace Stevens. But where is that influence now? To this question I can only offer a mournful reply: Emerson is alive, if hardly well, and living in *Forrest Gump*.

In this chapter I survey recent influential alternatives to the Gothic; some are beholden to Emerson, some not. We'll move backward chronologically, from the forms of facile transcendence that now dominate popular culture, to a lite form (it's not the only form) of 1960s transcendence, then on to modernism, a mode that, I think, has some of its origins in a desire to escape the Gothic. The chapter will take us from Forrest Gump, through Woodstock and *The Texas Chainsaw Massacre*, back to Jane Austen and T. S. Eliot. My objective is to show how, and why, Gothic's twentieth-century antagonists have failed. In doing so I hope to convey some sense of how strong the Gothic is in today's culture—as well, perhaps, as hinting at some vital alternatives to the Gothic vision.

"I'm Forrest, Forrest Gump." The film that swept the Academy Awards in 1994 chronicles the life of a golden-hearted dullard who sheds gentleness and light everywhere he goes. It's anything but a slasher movie; *Forrest Gump* is worlds away, it would seem, from *Silence of the Lambs*. Thick-tongued, ill-dressed Forrest, played by Tom Hanks, has the benevolent, faraway look of someone whose life was changed for good when small antennaed men took him up for a ride in their saucer, let him gaze on the earth from a great height, and taught him that all that lives is holy and all that happens is for the best.

Bad things frequently do happen to Forrest, but he survives them unscathed. His father takes off before he's born; as a boy he's trapped in leg braces so clunkingly awkward that Charles Dickens would have sent them back to the prop room; the love of Forrest's life snubs and snubs him; he goes to Vietnam and sees the carnage; his mother dies; the love of his life finally surrenders to him, then dies (of a "virus").

Through it all Alabaman Forrest is magnolia sweet. He runs fast (after kicking off the leg braces one lucky day) and plays for Bear Bryant on the Crimson Tide; he swings a mean ping-pong paddle and meets a president in recognition of his mastering that high art. With some slick technology, the movie manages to insert Hanks in newsreel footage of chief executives and other American potentates from past decades.

And of course Forrest gets rich. Everything his innocent hands touch turns to gold: there's a shrimp company and a lucky investment in Apple computers. Forrest is shyly wise and given to platitudes: "Life [is] like a box of chocolates; you never know what you're going to get." In answer to aspersions on his intelligence, he's prone to reply, "Stupid is as stupid does."

America loved it. The movie, which (no surprise) took a long time for a major studio to agree to produce, was a shock-top-hit. It grossed a fortune. It won all the awards and stole the heart of the heart of the country. The moral, I suppose, is that it's good to be sweet and dumb and self-effacing; it's good in itself, plus fate will reward you for it with fat checks. America underscored that wisdom by rewarding the film—dumb, sweet, and unremarkable—in the same way that the film contrived to reward Forrest. QED. Or at the very least it's pleasing to entertain such possibilities for the space of 142 minutes, while Forrest waits at a bus stop and narrates his life, with copious flashbacks, for all who care to loaf with him for a while.

At the core of *Forrest Gump* is the sugary fiction that dull virtue in tandem with humble, unresenting poverty is well rewarded. Accordingly, the many who are poor and unrewarded must not be virtuous, and those Americans who have been rewarded, or are about to be, must be good (and wondrously appealing), though maybe not so dull. Mostly the idea is that America, despite a few wayward incidents, is still a grand place to live, and that sweetness matters here more than wielding a sharp Darwinian claw. It takes a heart of stone to love *Forrest Gump*.

Surely, then, *Forrest Gump* is anything but a slasher movie. Though Forrest and his Ma reside in a Southern mansion turned boarding-house, there's no hint of haunting anywhere. In fact, many of America's historical traumas from the past forty years take place within Forrest's ken, sometimes close up. But he's completely unscathed. The major '60s assassinations punctuate the film; Forrest is on the scene in Vietnam; he's there when George Wallace tries to bar black students from the University of Alabama: sorrows track him.

The love of his life—who has the sense to resist Forrest's insipid charm for most of the film—undergoes all the shocks. She's into drugs and crazy sex; she gets the "virus." She's like the picture of Dorian Gray, recording ravages of the '60s and beyond, while Forrest, with his drooler's grin, stays clean. By the end of the movie the love's a sorry wreck, walking state's evidence against the Age of Aquarius. But Forrest has got what Edmund Burke called an "inexperiencing nature." Nothing blacks his hopeful disposition—which, presumably, is what makes him so lovable.

And if we all love Forrest, or most of us do, what sense can there be in talking about a culture of Gothic? Does terror truly reign in the land of *Forrest Gump?* Can a book about American Gothic now be apropos of anything much?

My answer is this. *Forrest Gump* played large in America in considerable part because it worked as a vacation, a few hours away from more pressing Gothic fears. Many of us believe—as Freud and his pop disciple Oprah Winfrey do, though in their different ways—that we're made what we are by traumas. We're all, to the current common understanding, damaged goods. Maybe we can't remember what it was that wrecked us. (The more wrecked our state the less likely we are to recall the horror.) But a major accident, a head-on with fate, that we walked away from as a ghost of our best potential self is back there in many of our secret annals. For Freud, it's the complex violence of the Oedipal encounter; for Oprah, it's often some kind of abuse.

Abuse is an intriguing word now: it covers a panoply of troubling events, from abrasive criticism ("shaming") to outright incest or rape. But you know that when someone says, in sotto voce conversation, that he or she was abused as a child, that there had best be respectful, nearly sanctified, silence. Don't ask, "What happened?"

When trauma looms centrally in your self-conception, one abiding question must be this: What would I have been without that damning accident? Why, you'd be innocent, charismatic, and rich, naturally. If the question is what does a trauma-free past look like—and feel like—the answer is Forrest Gump. Giving oneself over to Forrest for a couple of hours, one experiences the freedom of a life without trauma.

What needs to be underlined is the fact that the spirit of *Forrest Gump* isn't simply the inverse of the spirit that propels Poe's tales and *Silence of the Lambs*. Rather it's that *Gump* teems with potential traumas, teems with events conducive to lifelong terror. So *Gump* isn't just escapism; it contains within it—but denies the power of—all the Gothic pressures that it would let us evade.

———————————

Like contemporary Gothic, the current culture of easy transcendence can be divided into different forms. The sort provided by a film like *Forrest Gump* I'll simply call *pop transcendence,* in recognition of its general accessibility and of its promise that the changes will be effected at lightning speed. Pop transcendence, of which I'll give a number of other examples, is nearly as commonplace, though far less plausible, than contemporary terror Gothic (the mode exemplified by Ann Rice's novels, *Silence of the Lambs,* and renderings of the Simpson case); and in fact images of easy transcendence often act as antidotes, usually only partially successful, to pressing Gothic fears. Gothic shades tend to fall along their edges.

A second mode of easy transcendence is the one that I call the *therapeutic sublime.* The therapeutic sublime focuses on the inner self and provides an upbeat alternative to the interior Gothic mode largely created by Freud. As propounded by the likes of John Bradshaw and Robert Bly, the therapeutic sublime dramatizes various relatively facile strategies of self-rebegetting. Treatises on the therapeutic sublime show us how we might be transformed from our current unsatisfactory selves to paragons of wisdom, strength, sensitivity, and what have you. Though it is the easiest of the modes of facile transcendence to ridicule, I argue that the therapeutic sublime nonetheless often shows evidence of praiseworthy human desires for change.

The third style of contemporary Gothic, apocalyptic Gothic, seems to me to have few, if any, correlatives in the realms of easy transcendence. Where in the Gothic realm there is discourse on AIDS, plague, ecological disaster, and many other modes of future destruction, there is, from the regions of easy transcendence, little by way of reply. Utopian discourse is at what may be an all-time low in premillennial America. One might turn to predictions about the brave new world of cyberspace, as offered by the Tofflers, Nicholas Negroponte, and other corporate functionaries, I suppose. But such blithe auguries have few subscribers. Newt Gingrich's meanderings about waking up to a wall-sized, high-definition TV that shows the surf off Maui, about the home cyberoffice (no more commuting), and, for every illness, the computer-run home diagnostic chair, add up to little when set beside the prevailing visions of Gothic destruction that emanate now from every medium, and chiefly from TV (that pleasant surf will be a tidal wave by news time).[2]

In the sections that follow, I describe a number of the currently operative modes of easy transcendence, chronicle their relation to the culture of Gothic, and begin to suggest how they might contribute to some more arduous, and valuable, modes of cultural renovation.

Forrest Gump is framed by a feather. It starts with a sweet bit of white fluff winding slowly to earth, coasting on the wind, and ends with the feather's return as Forrest guides his little boy—not stupid, we're assured—onto the school bus. It's a testament to the movie's weight, that feather. But maybe too the feather is falling from heaven, shed by an angel, maybe Forrest's heavenly guardian. (On one occasion, Forrest claims heaven to be his certain destination.) Forrest's is a world in which angels would tread easily, for it's the ostensible inverse of Freddy Krueger's and Hannibal Lecter's, where you're guilty when you sin, and guilty when you don't.

In fact, watching *Forrest Gump* could precipitate one's need for the likes of Freddy. In a sequel to the first *Nightmare on Elm Street, Dream Warriors,* there's a sentimentally portrayed kid confined to a wheelchair, a kid cripple like the young Forrest. He's the type who lives for marathon games of Dungeons and Dragons. The kids who get slashed in this one are all perceptibly devoted to one or another illusion. They're addicted to fictions that seem to them worldly and tough, but aren't nearly as nasty as the base-line facts of Elm Street life, as embodied by Freddy (and their parents). When the sweet kid in the wheelchair, magus in his own mind, zaps Freddy once ("I am the Wizard-master," he declaims. "In the name of Lorick, Prince of Elves, demon be gone"), we're rooting for his D&D imagination to overwhelm the monster. (And of course a kid in a wheelchair has got to win; we adore cripples in films—when they turn up at your elbow at a party, it's often a different story.) But Freddy, with a mighty laugh, gestures to the kid's chair and lets him know that it's a better emblem for his scurrying-rat psyche than the wizard's cape. "I'm sorry, kid. I don't believe in fairy tales," bellows fictive Krueger, then applies the claw. If Craven wants to shock the American cult of air and light, he could do worse than put Forrest and Freddy together. Do you believe in fairy tales? In angels? Do you believe in Forrest?

Angels, for a while, were everywhere in America. Recent articles in hundreds of publications have affirmed that the great majority of Americans believe in angels and imagine that these heavenly creatures are there to protect them and others among the helpless. Angels can post at our bidding over land and ocean, collapsing time, annulling space. In 1990 there came *A Book of Angels* by Sophy Burnham, reciting tales of angelic intervention, including the one about the angel who, dressed like a skier in black, saves multiple lives. In the 1993 volume *Where Angels Walk,* the angels began dressing in white, but their purpose was the life-saving same. *Brush of an Angel's Wing* was still another big angel-to-the-rescue book; and though the pace has slowed down, the testimonials continue to come. Angels will be with us until well into the millennium.

When at the end of 1993 *Time* magazine asked America how it felt about angels, 69 percent claimed to believe in them.[3] Nearly half of us take ourselves to have a guardian angel of our own. What such creatures are up to when we maim ourselves and others no one seems eager to say. Even the American clergy, generally receptive to any sign of awakening spirituality, views the angel craze askance. America's current angels are fluffy creatures, flown off the fronts of greeting cards. In the Bible, they're beings of another order: an encounter with an angel transforms life—puts one on a harder, higher path. An angel announces Jesus' birth to Mary, bringing joy but also terrible woe; Jacob wrestles with an angel to secure God's blessing and leaves the encounter with a wound that makes him limp the rest of his days; an angel stays Abraham's hand when he's about to sacrifice his son.

By contrast, our current angels are wisps of good luck, the spiritual equivalent of smiley faces. As Harold Bloom put it, "Our passion for angels is not surprising in a nation where one of the ongoing mottoes is 'God's country and mine!' If God loves us individually, then it follows that most of us should have an angel of her or his own. To find your angel is not necessarily to find yourself, though most quests for the angel seem nowadays to suppose that a guardian angel is rather more like a dog or a cat than like a husband or a wife. You acquire an angel in the expectation that this addition to your household will give you perpetual and unconditional love."[4]

An angel is nearly the diametrical opposite of a Gothic villain. One of the archetypes for all Gothic villains, Milton's

Satan, begins as an angel and after his fall is often compared to his former brightly winged self. Our current angels are pure good, completely clean, unambiguously on our side. The Gothic hero-villain has a bright allure (he's one of the elect), but that allure functions of course as a deception. The angel shines and is as good and un-self-interested as he is attractive.

What I'm suggesting is that if you're used to Gothic villains—to pondering the serial killer, the child molester, the brilliant psychopath, the man-monster—as cultural archetypes, then you may find a certain relief among the angels. These figures are just too wispy and insubstantial to make much sense in themselves, as something that adults could entertain the idea of believing in. Polls aside, I'm not sure they actually do much more than that. But angels do make sense when they're seen as providing a kind of mental vacation, temporary deliverance from a culture loaded with images of Gothic terror.

And the crises from which the angels are supposed to deliver their various beneficiaries are of a certain familiar type. Angels swoop down to save us from strange, undiagnosable diseases; from maladies like cancer that possess the body; from mysterious, sudden dangers; from persecution and pursuit. In other words, angels have a special proclivity for helping us out of Gothic fixes. Like *Gump*, the angel tale often works not just by giving us a vacation from Gothic, but also by invoking and then redeeming us from Gothic terrors.

Every angel in good standing delivers one thing: a miracle. They come on to grab our loved ones from out of the mouth of death. They deliver a new lease on life. What's the function of this kind of lite religion? Why do ostensibly sane people seem to require it? If *Forrest Gump* annuls trauma and gives us an idealized dip unaffected by horror in any form, the angel craze goes a step further. A miracle is exactly the inverse of a trauma. A miracle is the unearned lucky break, just as the trauma is the undeserved tragedy. And we must—mustn't we?—have justice in life. If we are damaged and deformed by trauma, there must be a counterweight somewhere in the universe.

Samuel Johnson once observed that in every life pain is guaranteed; we'll all suffer, no matter who we are. Whereas there are lives, many of them, in which no real joy ever comes to pass. Recall the wisdom of Silenus, the satyr who told King Midas what human happiness was: "The best," said Silenus, "is never to be born; next best is to die early." For such wisdom—which is rugged and banal, not exaltingly sensationalistic like Gothic pessimism—we as a culture have no appetite. We want pop transcendence: bread and circuses, angels and *Forrest Gump*.

American culture is now jammed like a Christmas pie with all kinds of self-aggrandizing sweets. As well as being loaded with Gothic plots, from Stephen King to the news at noon, our culture also contains a plethora of forms that are absolutely opposed to the Gothic. Everywhere there are being hawked facile brands of transcendence, the kind of things that Gothic hopelessness can compel one to wish for. Recipes for facile transcendence are likely to be commonplace in a culture where many people un-self-consciously think of themselves as Gothic victims. If you're persuaded that some trauma, massive if perhaps unremembered, is at the root of your present misery, then it stands to reason that you'll hope for an antithetical event, comparably grand, to reverse matters and right your course. While Emily St. Aubert is imprisoned at Montoni's Udolpho, she whiles her time away concocting implausible, if titillating, fantasies about her eventual rescue, and her glamorous rescuer.

Productions like *Forrest Gump* and the angel books invert the Gothic. But in another sense facile transcendence reinforces the culture of terror. The very insubstantiality of the easy transcendence scenarios, their status, acknowledged even by some of their consumers, as simple wish fulfillment, testifies to the absence of plausible hope for many Americans. The fact that the devotees of easy transcendence—the self-help programs, the spiritual journeys, the New Age philosophies—move so rapidly from one to another, as though an endless carousel, a spiritual lazy Susan, were forever turning, and know that they will leave channeling for primal-scream therapy, and screaming for orgone treatment, suggests the despair that often underlies the current quest for self-renovation.

In even a condensed survey of currently operative forms of pop transcendence, we ought not to overlook some of the more obvious cases. Take for example the culture of TV in its non-Gothic guise. For as well as hard-wiring anxiety into its viewers with ongoing horror fare, TV also offers a mode of very low-key transcendence. It teaches the capacity to lift yourself above the mere contingency of life. In fact, TV shows you a way to overcome the Gothic fear that it so assiduously works to instill. One might call the philosophy in question TV Zen mastery (or maybe the art of medium cool). David Letterman is its major exemplar.

In Letterman, viewers find a hipper self. He's someone who indeed watches lots of TV—you can't understand his jokes without being well-immersed in the medium—but is always superior to it. So part of what Letterman teaches is how to spend hours glued to the tube and to feel good about it: to feel good about yourself, as the current idiom has it. By getting his jokes you pass the exam. (His persona is that of an ultra-cool prof.)

In general TV makes a pact with its viewers. What it usually won't do is confront its audience with ideas or images that challenge their limits. It must never make the audience insecure, must always make us feel in control. An acquaintance of mine, writing for an avant-garde type TV series, got into one of the fights of his professional life when he tried to insert an unattributed line of Melville's into the dialogue. "But the audience will be confused": his bosses knew that what even the smartest TV watchers generally want is the feeling of complete mastery, of knowing everything that's going on, all the time.

Letterman modifies that. On his show, there are jokes you might not get. But the main reason for not getting his jokes, for not acing the test, is insufficient acquaintanceship with TV or the world of entertainment overall. (Sometimes Dave even *mocks* TV, gumming the hand that feeds him.) TV has finally found a way to challenge its viewers, to make things feel edgy, but in doing so it's enhanced its hold rather than undermining it.

By looking at Letterman, you test your knowingness (can I be as dismissive as Dave?) and learn new standards for TV cool. The angel craze and ambitious New Age offerings promise high-buzz pop transcendence—you're supposed to leap over your prior, lowly self into something new. But there's also a smug and cool pop transcendence. Marshall McLuhan taught that to survive on TV, you have to be low-key, wary, ironic. To survive and prosper in a culture where TV is king, you have to be similarly armored, lightly but sturdily protected.

Much of the interest on Letterman revolves around testing Dave's cool and thus raising the standard. Madonna said fuck, and fuck again to try to shock Dave (and didn't entirely fail). Another guest hiked her shirt and showed the guru what was underneath. The show went to England, which is to low-key hip what India is to spirituality, and it brought on Dave's mom. Can Dave continue to be cool even as his mother reveals childhood secrets? (Tune in.) Could he survive an on-camera enema, equanimity intact? (Maybe, maybe.) Dave is an up-scale, ironic Forrest Gump: nothing can touch him.

So you too can presumably learn to survive all sorts of indignities without doing one of the things that's sure to sink you in current professional culture: showing naked emotion, making Dave ashamed of you. Like Dave, you can learn to greet any expression of enthusiasm—excitement for a new idea, a fresh way of doing things, a new vision—with the laid-back contempt it surely deserves. You'll never be taken in and you'll never be humiliated. As Northrop Frye says, of all the ways of conducting life, "expertly conventional behavior is the most difficult to mock."

In general, two kinds of guests appear on Letterman's show: the celebrities, who banter with Dave in equally ironic, equally empty terms; and the plebeians, who are objects of ridicule. First the plebes were featured accompanying their pets in the Stupid Pet Trick sequences: dog attacks vacuum cleaner on command, owner cheers absurdly, etc. But then the show took a sophisticated step forward—and found its essence—when Stupid Pet Tricks morphed into Stupid Human Tricks.

Dave from Boston spins around in a clothes dryer and changes his shirt; Dave from TV looks on in mock-genial derision. On comes Scott from West Chester, Pennsylvania, a hot dog salesman by day and a bartender by night. Scott has brought an electric fan with him. What will he do with it? He'll stop its rotation with his tongue. Scott has a big tongue, a potent one, too, as we see, once in live action, once in slo-mo replay, when he sticks it way out and forces it against the whizzing fan blade. The fan freezes, Scott's tongue pressed grotesquely against the metal, looking like fresh beef liver. Letterman gives his boyish hateful look, part Tom Sawyer, part Ranthar, King of the Fire Lizards. "Nice of Scott to drop by and make us all sick." Poor Scott. But of course there's no escape. Of the ten reasons proffered for watching Letterman on one of the show's Top Ten Lists, number ten is this: "When you're not watching the show, we're making fun of you."

Letterman quite simply is the spirit of at least half of TV, the spirit to which America often aspires. He teaches us, to adapt a phrase from Mark Crispin Miller, how to see the joke lest we ourselves become it (that threat being the downside of TV transcendence). Another way to make the point is to say that Letterman contributes to the spirit that presides over that distinctly American creation, the sitcom. As the Olympian Gods looked down on the doings of puny humans, so we are invited to look upon the players on sitcom TV. They have so many problems. And they're always so agitated. They're obsessives. Why can't they relax, see that it's no big deal, and that all will be well by the half hour's end? The sitcom teaches detachment, superiority. It lets us feel in control in the world. (Lord, what fools these mortals be.) It's Dave's domain. When Dave's ratings begin to flag, it will perhaps be because he's taught his lesson in cool well enough, and that the audience would prefer to exercise their prowess in low-grade accommodating contempt on entities like the solicitous Jay Leno.

Having put on Dave's cool for watching TV, one is in a position to watch Gothic fare with apparent equanimity. None of that murder and mayhem, blood and slasher fare gets to me; it's just images, just stuff they jam between the commercials. But a false urbanity is a porous defense. TV and other media can commune all the more effectively with emotional life, with dream life, when a programmatic, rather than a supply-responsive irony is in gear. TV mastery, which would seem the reverse of hunger for TV Gothic, may actually open the way for more saturating doses of fear.

Maybe what makes Dave's show a titillation is his habit of putting his celebrity at risk. He dares his guests to do something that will turn him into a mere audience member, one of the unwashed (one of the unmediated). Celebrity, it's been said, entails the maintenance of a primary narcissism, a cool outer perfection that's never ruffled. Narcissism puts a bright sheen on the self. Celebrities, perhaps, are people who can appear never to have left what Lacan calls the mirror stage, the stage when the image in the glass is all that one could ever want. And celebrities exert charisma; they pull us toward them whether we like it or not.

Camille Paglia describes the charismatic allure thus: "Charisma is the numinous aura around a narcissistic personality. It flows outward from a simplicity or unity of being and a composure and controlled vitality. There is gracious accommodation, yet commanding impersonality. Charisma is the radiance produced by the interaction of male and female elements in a gifted personality. The charismatic woman has a masculine force and severity. The charismatic man has an entrancing female beauty. Both are hot and cold, glowing with presexual self love."[5] Maybe we want such self-enclosed perfection for ourselves. Freud said that our love for our children is in part a reawakening of our own primary narcissism; we'll do almost anything to recapture it. It seems that we all want to go back to the beginning, when we were our own perfect Eden.

But why is it that charismatic figures, after extended contact, become so demoralizing? Why are there few things more depressing than the charismatic friend we made three months ago? Maybe it's because we inevitably see that the anointed one, whom we thought might share the aura, doesn't need or care about us at all. We're revealed then as just an interchangeable audience member who has nothing in common with the celebrity and her glittering world. Perhaps the letdown involves our having to recognize ourselves as another face in the crowd, the condition from which the celebrity seemed to promise deliverance, pop transcendence.

So maybe celebrity offers, through identification, a quick lift out of the quotidian self, the fantasy of a new pride and potency. But that fantasy then needs to be undone, so that we're not the ones left stranded. We need to do it to the celebrities before they do it to us. On the checkout line at every supermarket one encounters the debunking mechanism that keeps the celebrity wheel turning, the tabloids. The tabloids tell all; they dish you the dirt. Is Liz Taylor the most gorgeous woman in the world, our Cleopatra, ageless in her beauty, and a grand partisan in the anti-AIDS wars to boot? Ah, but let us consider her eating disorders, the binge and bloat, her multiple marriages, the rumors of depression, grief, sorrow, and pills and pills.

As Lacan remarks, neurosis is the perception that somewhere there are others who are genuinely happy. And those, presumably, are the stars, whom we alternate identifying with (Roseanne's got it right, I don't give a fuck about anybody—I'll do it my own way), and cheer the denigration of (that slut, she had it coming to her). Inflation and deflation: the return and the defeat of narcissism. Hollywood is a major mock-transcendence industry. And since Hollywood movies now are just about exclusively star vehicles, the building up of the image is one of their chief functions. To have an image, to be coherent and self-contained, apparently dependent on no one for self-identity, that is the star's role.

The tabloids are, in effect, the Gothic underside of the pop-transcendence, celebrity phenomenon. In the tabs, you meet the darker selves of the celebrities who have captivated you. You learn that they cheat, grub for money, trash their friends; they grasp like babies for whatever goodies roll by. In the tabloids and on the tabloid TV shows, you meet the star's doppelgangers and have the pleasure of throwing down—preliminary to again raising, as from the dead—the current Olympians. The phenomenon of celebrity, which looks at first like sheer pop transcendence, has a streak of Gothic running through it.

But perhaps the fans (short, of course, for fanatics), the seekers after celebrity, are looking for something better. As well as Paglia's Hollywood Babylon version, there are other accounts of charisma. There is, for instance, Max Weber's. To Weber charisma derives from deeds, from making a difference in the world. It's the property of miracle workers, prophets, and teachers. (The early Christian meaning of charisma associates it with the power to heal or to speak in tongues.) And perhaps the disciples of great teachers do receive some of the balm, as Christ's twelve followers are said to have done. But film and TV stars have nothing to transfer. They know little, can do little. Is our fascination with them a displaced religious fascination? Is it a hunger for the truths that a great teacher or a secular prophet can convey? In our ritual of throwing down celebrities, reconceiving them as Gothic hero-villains, are we expressing anger at them for not living up to our hopes for inspired leadership and enlarging instruction?

In symbiotic play with the culture of celebrity is the culture of advertisement, another current realm of pop transcendence. One might in fact see the entertainment industry as a set of production sites, of image factories, geared to the making of celebrities. Those celebrities, charisma radiant, then act as attractive packaging and display devices for material goods, goods that are now likely to be produced in factories offshore. Perhaps in the global economy of twenty years hence, America will find its major role as packager and promoter of the world's commodities.

America's preeminent media critic, Mark Crispin Miller, has described the harsh contemporary culture of advertisement as something much different from the advertising cosmos of two and three decades ago. Miller notes how the billboard and magazine ads of the 1960s tended toward a certain debased pastoralism. You enjoyed your Kool cigarette in the company of others, in blissful repose out in nature, surrounded by grass and trees. But things have changed. Now the archetypal advertising figure is the isolated individual, exuding power. He's supercharged on his can of Schlitz Malt Liquor; high on Gatorade; empowered by Marlboros to heave his woman like a steer across his shoulders and be off with her. He's the wild gangsta rapper, sucking powerfully on his bottle and selling well in the wealthy white suburbs of Long Island.

Miller puts matters harshly, but not inaccurately: "While the brand name may vary from ad to ad, all . . . are unified by their promotion of the same bad creed: that 'power' is all, that it means nothing more than dominating others, and that you must therefore have that 'power' or end up broken by it." And, Miller goes on, while advertising's techniques have become "ever flashier, speedier, more ingenious and hypnotic, its pitch has gotten more mean-minded and invidious, as it has come to ask us not—as the ads had done for decades—to take it easy for a moment, to lose ourselves in some edenic little pleasure, often sharing it with others, but only to stand out, to come first, to take what you want, and take it now: to be the lone, hard, self-indulgent center of attention, wondrously 'empowered' by car or pudding, pain-killer or panty-hose, shoes or wristwatch, mouthwash or CD player, no less than by your latest Newport or this can of Bud. In short, whatever edible or gadget it may be promoting, advertising now tends to sell it by promoting no physical or social enjoyment whatsoever (an experience with some slight utopian implication), but only by identifying it with that icy, narcissistic posture that looks so good within the ads themselves."[6]

It is of course no coincidence that the kind of power that the ads tout is also the power implicitly claimed by the celebrity of the present. And by the new-mold rock star, the kid with an attitude, James Dean of our current disorder, who outrages the old archons, going for it all and living large, taking shit from no one but manager, producer, video director, and whoever else markets him, down to the flacks who sell the consignment T-shirts and caps, and from which (such is the system) some bands take the bulk of their profits.

The road of pop power-transcendence has a particular allure for women in fin-de-siècle America. In *The Beauty Myth*, Naomi Wolf describes a rather disturbing, and currently prevalent, female persona: the aloof ice-woman, sexually self-contained, cruel, remote, perfect. She too stares at you from the provinces of advertisement—all self-enclosed self-love, daring women to achieve her invulnerability, goading men to break her down. Wolf observes that as women entered the work force in the '70s, the matter of what they would need and desire as more broadly enfranchised players became a major issue. "The feminine sexual style of the 1960s," Wolf says, "was abandoned in popular culture, because for women to be sexual in that way—cheerfully, sensually, playfully, without violence or shame, without dread of the consequences—would break down completely institutions that were tottering crazily enough since women had changed merely their *public* roles."[7] Break down completely? I'm not sure. But it certainly is the case that women were encouraged—one might even say compelled—to conform to the canons of male professional identity when they entered the higher echelons of work.

At the same time, says Wolf, the supposedly perfect female body was on display everywhere, providing a harsh standard against which women were to measure their own allure. "Soon," Wolf writes, "'perfection' was represented as a woman's 'sexual armor,' made more urgent an achievement in the 1980s when AIDS intensified an atmosphere that suggested to women that only an inhuman beauty would lead a man to risk his life for sex."[8]

Laura Mulvey has argued that throughout much of mainstream cinema, the arrival of a beautiful, mysterious woman on the scene—a femme fatale—signals the beginning of a quest.[9] ("Who's that girl?" sings Madonna, about herself of course.) She will need to be pursued, investigated, sussed out until she's fully known and dominated. (Hitchcock's *Vertigo*, the film that tells the tale of poor height-frightened Scottie, obsessively pursuing beautiful blond Madeline, his quest leading to her death, is a cinema archetype here.) The ice maiden brings on her own destruction at the hands of the angry, perplexed man. Thus an apparently feminist icon, the self-sufficient femme fatale, provokes a reaction that undermines feminism's central drive, the drive for equality and independence.

The pop transcendent personae that we've identified with the help of Wolf and Miller serve a doubly inhibiting purpose. Mere wish-fulfillment in themselves, they can nonetheless absorb the urge for more productive and creative forms of self-realization. Nonnutritional stuff, they swell the belly nonetheless. Such personae are appealing in that they require no self-exertion to adopt, just the purchase of the right products (though tomorrow you'll have to buy more and different ones). Thus they can displace the attractions of more arduous forms of self-renewal that might be met with in art and political activism at their best.

And because they superficially resemble more genuine forms of self-creation, the pop transcendent personae act to discredit them in advance. Authentic self-remaking (of which more later) is rendered potentially absurd by its proximity to the debased simulations. The staged self-reliance of the rock star makes the genuinely independent and costly gesture of the corporate whistle-blower glow less cleanly than it should. Thus the images Miller and Wolf identify impoverish both immediate life and future possibilities.

And they work effectively by posing themselves on the border of the Gothic: our pop heroes now tend to resemble hero-villains. They exude danger, as well as exerting attraction. Even the ideal personae that turn up in our ads and films smack of evil; created within the delimiting conventions of Gothic, they have nothing to teach, or even intimate, about the complex good of which some people, some of the time, have shown themselves capable.

But can one seriously inveigh against television, celebrity, advertising? They're our Blatant Beasts (to borrow a name from Spenser): aren't they so blatant, in fact, that all of us, or all of us who matter, see right through them? I'd suggest that it's by being so overbearing that they are, in effect, largely criticism-proof. What serious person would stoop to pointing out how absurd, how inane, time-wasting, and empty TV generally is? But the fact that TV and its kindred cultural spirits are so egregious is part of what preserves them. Their sheer obnoxiousness renders intelligent response nearly untenable. Yet TV, celebrity creation, and ads now contribute massively to the cultural weather in which most of us live out our lives. Saying that they don't count—or they don't count for people like me and my sophisticated friends—is the purest hubris.

The forms of pop transcendence that I've mentioned so far can function as escapes from the more deeply felt pressures of the Gothic vision, of terror and despair. *Forrest Gump,* angels, celebrities, power ads, TV Zen mastery, celebrity vehicle films, these things are installments in the history of advertising, or not much more than that. And of course there are many other kindred forms active in 1990s American culture. What I've offered here is just a partial list. A more comprehensive survey would have time for phenomena like the self-help movement, twelve-step programs (or most of them), Prozac,

TV sports, Las Vegas (capital of facile transcendence), being born again, EST, automobile culture, magazines, most pop music—the list would never end.

Yet there are other forms of promised renovation in American culture that compel greater interest, at least on my part. Oddly enough, these are the forms that have most often been maligned by intellectuals. Today, academics tend to demonstrate their progressive credentials by championing this or that piece of mass culture: heavy metal, Madonna, punk rock, hip-hop, rap, whatever. But the forms of renovation that obviously display the vulnerability and spiritual need of those who gravitate toward them, such forms are often too disturbing for the academic mind to regard calmly.

Consider Robert Bly's best-selling *Iron John,* the book at the heart of the so-called men's movement. Iron John is a sort of male mother, and the image isn't entirely unappealing. He's "an ancient hairy man," the necessary complement, Bly claims, to the young man of sensibility, the feminized male, who came out of '60s pacifism and developed under the influence of the women's movement.[10] Such a man, for all his receptivity and empathic power, has trouble connecting with his own passions (anger is bad, ambition is bad bad) and living with concentration. He lacks resolve. (In some regards, Bill Clinton, intelligent and compassionate but without the toughness to take unpopular stands, fits the image.) Given that there are very few lines in Bly's psychological sketch—it's too reductive to satisfy for long—it's still apt enough and reasonably well executed. At the very least, the readers who flocked to the book recognized something of themselves in Bly's portrait, which is, if gently conveyed (the preeminent nurturing male mother in the book is Bly himself), still critical enough.

Bly's larger point is the rather simple but not inconsequential one that you do not necessarily need to choose between strength and sensitivity, between self-reliance and humanity.

Bly seems to me right that one effect of the women's movement has been to provide an array of self-making stories that women can draw on to conceive their own paths, while men—middle-class men, in particular—have left themselves in a relative vacuum. Hemingway won't do anymore surely, but guilt and shame over the past crimes of masculinity probably aren't sound, exclusive bases for male *Bildung,* either.

Andrew Ross urbanely suggests that Iron John—beefy, muscular, bearded, kind—might remind one of a piece of gay pseudo-rough-trade.[11] Point taken. But in Bly's more effective evocations—and Bly is a poet of some gifts—Iron John summons up a more affecting American archetype: Walt Whitman, the wound-dresser. During the Civil War, Whitman worked without pay as a male nurse, treating the wounded in the hospitals around Washington, offering no more care to Union soldiers than to Confederates. The greatest American poet went among the lowliest, spending his pathetic income on presents for the men, tobacco and candy, paper and stamps. He transcribed their letters home. He joked with them while they were healing; he held them as they died.

Supremely gentle, delicate in both his person and his work, Whitman was also a surpassingly tough man. He wrote what he wished and as he wished. His poetry is sexual, eccentric, prophetic, and wild. For his pains, he got censored, excoriated, and also, on occasion, praised by some of the best writers in America (himself included: Whitman reviewed his own books more than once). The man's courage was, and is, nearly beyond praise.

Iron John, whatever his cartoonish excesses, is a statement against conformity, a call to embrace a more confident self, to stand up for yourself and speak your truth, as Whitman did and paid for doing. That is also what the '60s taught at its best—and *Iron John* is in some ways a book of the '60s. One of the best things to come out of that much-demonized period was a reburnishing of the Emersonian and Whitmanian belief that you ought never to shut up, at least when you have a strong conviction. "A firm perswasion," Blake says, is what makes a prophet. One ethos of the '60s entailed standing up to oppressive power and sounding off, from Mario Savio and the Berkeley Free Speech Movement to Bob Dylan, who continues on in the vein.

A passage from Bly on the spirit of Hermes addresses this matter of truth-telling (which is something different from promulgating Truth) well enough:

Sometimes when friends are talking in a closed room, the heat of the conversation begins to increase: witty things are said; contributions flow from all sides; leaps of imagination appear; the genuinely spiritual follows an instant after the genuinely obscene. Hermes has arrived . . . Hermes is magical, detail-loving, obscene, dancelike, goofy, and not on a career track.[12]

Academia, which is now more and more one constricting career track, provides precious little of such exchange. Self-censorship is the order of the day.

One notable thing about the 1960s ethos of free speech is that it didn't all come out a desire to breed sweetness and shed light: there's also the wish to deliver a telling blow. A witch in one of Frost's poems says that she never could resist the prospect of doing good when it let her pull off something malicious at the same time. ("Right's right, and the temptation to do right / When I can hurt someone by doing it / Has always been too much for me, it has.")[13] In the manner of Jimi Hendrix's marvelous deconstruction of "The Star Spangled Banner," an admixture of love and rage directed at free, murderous, imperial America, the ethos of truth-telling often involves aggression. When Dylan, the greatest of the '60s prophets, says that he was older once, but younger than that now, he's taking aim at the members of his audience who have gone over to being authorities themselves. He refuses to flatter his followers by setting up a club comprising people who know what's happening.

Dylan has always conveyed a good deal of pain and loneliness in his songs, and it's honesty about such things that Bly lacks, and that probably helped make his book such a prolific best-seller. (Dylan can't fill the big halls anymore.) Bly is unwilling to take the problem of conformity seriously. He never admits that if you get into the Iron John mode at your job, it's quite likely that by the end of the week you won't have one. Then, in time, you can be Iron John living in a refrigerator box or out of the back seat of your car. The sublime vision of Iron John, without concomitant reflection on the social arrangements that inhibit it and many other worthy ideals, too, amounts to a lot of fine dancing in the dark.

Society has little time at present (did it ever?) for people who act in the way that Bly commends. And though it's in many ways noble enough, Bly's therapeutic sublime is, like the inane men's groups that it helped to spawn, a weekend thing. On Saturday and Sunday, you can be a sensitive warrior, as you page through *Iron John*. But during the week you'd best go back to being Mister Jones, out of Dylan's "Ballad of a Thin Man": something's happening here and you don't know what it is. Or if you do, you probably shouldn't let on.

Women Who Run with the Wolves by Clarissa Pinkola Estés (Ph.D.) is in many ways the female version of *Iron John*. *Wolves* has sold over a million copies, and for reasons that aren't hard to fathom.[14] Its image of the wild woman has got to be deeply appealing in a country that is asking women, particularly as they enter the middle-class professions in droves, to surrender whatever spiritual and erotic intensity they might have in return for the pleasures of corporate stability. Estés's wildwoman is the feminine equivalent of Bly's hairy man ("wet, dark, and low"), naturally, and she's probably as disconcerting to the male reader as Iron John is to women. (One measure of whether a work is a mere wish fulfillment, rather than something more demanding, something that might read and authentically change its reader, is whether its appeal is restricted to one sex or the other.)

Women Who Run with the Wolves shares the drawback of *Iron John*. If you do go back into the wildwoman, you're not likely, at least in sexist America, to do anything more than scare the man that you want half to death and persuade a few of your more credulous neighbors that you're a witch. But the book itself takes little note of such sorry facts. Just listen to all the stories about the vibrant, sexy, independent women, hair flaying the wind, those mythic mothers, then become one with them. (Paperback book, $15.95; tapes available for inspiration in transit, priced extra.)

———————

Or consider coming home to your inner child, the course commended by the best-selling therapist John Bradshaw. If your needs in infancy weren't met, says Bradshaw, your wounded inner infant is still present with all of her original energy and hope. Act now. Bradshaw's idea of a dialogue between self and inner child is manifest in a note that, the therapist claims, his own abandoned bantling wrote to him: "Dear John," it goes, "I want you to come get me I want to matter to someone. I don't want to be alone. Love, Little John."[15]

This inner correspondence may comprise the worst single swatch of prose published in America in 1992. And yet . . . And yet, slovenly and foolish though it is, it does begin to touch a vision of some value. Part of a humanistic education, a literary education, ought to be learning consciously to experience, and then to express, emotions. No less a personage than T. S. Eliot was willing to say that one function of poetry is to find words, however ambiguous, obscure, or complex, to evoke the range of feelings that lie unarticulated in most of us. At a moment when even literary education has dropped the cultivation of this power in the interest of a colder, more analytical approach, and where institutional culture is, as the members of the Frankfurt School predicted, growing progressively more abstract, efficient, and impersonal in its workings, it is no wonder that many of us have little access to our subtler life of feeling.

In popular culture, the cruder emotions are always on display. Turn on *Oprah* for high-intensity doses of rage, sorrow, longing, then more rage. But a crude popular culture gives little heed to more tender or subtle feelings. And one must begin somewhere.

Bradshaw is fond of quoting Wordsworth, another person fascinated with childhood, and yet Bradshaw's therapeutic engagement with childhood is quite unlike the poet's. To Wordsworth, the child is a source of potential vitality, but it's important not to identify entirely with that past self. To do so would mean living completely without defenses, opening yourself to ruin (as Wordsworth felt his friend Coleridge had done). Wordsworth is desperately attracted to the remembered child, because he knows that's where poetic power, the power to see nature afresh, without inhibitions, lies. And he'll get just close enough to imbibe such power without ruining himself. So Wordsworth takes some pains to negotiate and renegotiate his relation to the child that, like Bradshaw, he sees as abiding within.

If you try to become that child, as Bradshaw for all purposes recommends, the results will likely be that you'll regress into utter selfishness, maybe something worse. Or, recall Bly, that your sensitivity will make you incompatible—and outcast—in a world that doesn't value feeling much at all. What happens when the inner child, or even the person who has managed to restore some self-conscious emotional life through the exercises Bradshaw and his ilk commend, goes back to the office? Bradshaw can't—and won't—conceive of the tensions between the world as it is and the sensitivity he wants, rather naively, to restore.

In a well-known piece published in *Harper's*, the cultural critic David Rieff hit Bradshaw and the inner child/co-dependency movement with about all he had.[16] To Rieff, the desire to make contact with a prior being is a selfish, small-minded gesture: you ought to get out and get interested in politics and the planet's fate. Put the world's hungry children before the emotionally omnivorous inner infant.

One understands Rieff's impatience. But Rieff is so entirely unsympathetic to the motives of people who respond to the likes of Bradshaw that in a certain sense he confirms the therapist's major point. Rieff ices over in the face of all this talk about emotion. He doesn't get it. Rieff is unable to see the legitimate needs, needs for a life of feeling, that might prompt someone to embrace Bradshaw for want of something better. Puerile and narrow as it may be, Bradshaw's therapeutic sublime offers to break the inner dam. To respond to that offer honestly is no crime, though to make the offer in Bradshaw's jejune spirit may be something close.

When Frederick Crews looked into the Gothic scandal of recovered memory for the *New York Review of Books*, he rightly castigated the deceiving therapists who have encouraged their patients to cook up false memories. But Crews showed little interest in why someone's suffering might lead her to such outrageous claims for attention. What hurts these young women to make them cry out as they do? Why does being a daughter in America, in a good family, with ostensibly loving parents, still leave many fit for the hospital? Modernist sensibilities like Rieff's and Crews's want a cleaner, more cogent world than the one that is revealed by the likes of Bradshaw and the recovered-memory proponents—and, more subtly and truly, by Freud and Wordsworth.

Estés, Bly, and Bradshaw haven't got a full sense of resistance against which to measure their visionary hopes. They feel that what stops people from finding Iron John or the child within is ignorance, irrational fear. People are scared of change, scared to be emotionally vulnerable. But it's not just irrational worry that makes people unable to come into their own, even when they hear about some attractive way of doing so. For in actuality, such transformation will cost a good deal. Often we have responsibilities that would make the kind of change that Bly commends an act of some violence against people we cherish. The only job you can probably hold down as Bly's large-hearted and brave male mother is that of itinerant, workshop-holding poet-visionary, a job that seems already taken.

Bly and Bradshaw make it all look too easy. Reading their work, and books like Moore's *Care of the Soul*, and Redfield's *The Celestine Prophecy* and all the other spiritual manuals that decorate the bookstores, one wonders why humanity hasn't already ascended into heaven en masse. It all sounds so good and simple. But the books are vacations. You read them on the weekends and imagine yourself into the enlightened states they describe: you become more meditative, thoughtful, considerate, loving, sweet, tough, capable, whatever's in the recipe, but only until Monday morning or so.

What more sophisticated readers need to take account of is the fact that these books aren't as empty as their intellectual attackers can make them sound. Their popularity is evidence of people's craving for better lives, lives that actually have some humane design and some future purpose to them. And yet these visions of the therapeutic sublime so lack the true element of resistance to their vaunting hopes that they stand as little more than spiritual travel guides for those who never intend to leave home.

Bly and in some measure Bradshaw are creatures of the American 1960s: both are proponents of Rousseauian regression to nature. Become the child, become the wildman, throw off the trammels of civilization. So the culture of Woodstock affirmed pleasure, ease, and humane enjoyment: all good initial alternatives to a greedy, war-mongering society. Yet many members of the '60s generation wanted to stay forever in easy bliss—never leave the yellow submarine. Similarly, Bly and Bradshaw have no interest in using the move to a higher innocence (as William Blake might have called it) as a ground for confronting an unjust status quo. Unlike Dylan and Blake, they want to return to Beulah land and hang out there, get a little high, enjoy the good times, and never leave.

When Hendrix bent and blasted "The Star Spangled Banner" at Woodstock, he gave the audience pleasure *and* politics at the same time. But the ethos of both Woodstock and *Woodstock,* for most of the audience, in the mud and at the theater, was regression, pure melting away. The regressive legacy of the 1960s is still present—for some it's the '60s' only legacy—and still having its effects. This is particularly true among the young, for many of whom rock culture is something to tune into for sybaritic Friday and Saturday nights prior to putting on the Brooks Brothers outfit Monday morning.

When affirming the ethos of Woodstock becomes an end in itself, troubles set in. Woodstock Nation tends to deny darker energies (to Rousseau we're all born pure) and so leaves one all the more vulnerable to Gothic eruptions, something I want to demonstrate in this section with a compressed survey of some '60s modes of pop transcendence.

Easy transcendence in the '60s mode, cultural pleasure without politics, softens its adherents, making them ultimately more susceptible to institutional control. But such a version of pop transcendence does something else that's nefarious enough as well, something that's dramatized brilliantly in a very smart and nasty film of 1974 called *The Texas Chainsaw Massacre*. Whatever its production values, *TCM* (as those who love it say) manages very effectively to haunt the Age of Aquarius. The film is set in the Texas wasteland, where it's hot and dry and there are no vernal spirits to be found. Aquarius has set, and it's now, we're informed, the moment of Saturn, the god who presides over the Iron Age, the god who devours his children.

Children *are* devoured in *TCM;* four of the five young people whom we meet at the start of the film tooling through the wasteland in their passenger van, official vehicle of hippiedom, off rambling, looking for another installment of Woodstock, end up killed, dressed, and ready to eat. They're set upon by a crazy clan, an all-male family: Pop, who has some pretense to normality; Hitchhiker, an American psychopath; and Leatherface, three hundred or so pounds of jiggling baby fat, with butcher's apron, fright wig, and leather mask cut with holes for dulled-down eyes and slurping idiot's tongue (probing the air, looking for the nipple). Leatherface wields the chainsaw. (It's not clear whether one should count Grandpa in the family census; he comes to life only after sucking blood.)

The family used to work in the local slaughterhouse, but when automation came, they lost their jobs. Loony and dim, but not illogical exactly, they just kept doing what they were good at. Now they're a male tribe of cannibals, fending intrepidly for themselves against the world—*TCM* is a kind of mutant *Bonanza*.

I said that the young people were set upon by the family, which isn't exactly right. The youngsters make the first move. A couple heads off to take a ritualistic nude swim and finds—this isn't Woodstock, the film insists time and again—that the swimming hole has dried up completely. Saturn has usurped water-bearing Aquarius. Then the young man, seeing the outwardly well-maintained house up ahead, hits on an idea. He'll go over there and get some gasoline (the van is nearly out); for payment he'll leave them his guitar, then pick it up later.

A good deal of the young people's innocent hubris, their sense that all the world is hip, welcoming, and yours to ask for if you're just gentle and beautiful enough, is conveyed in the young man's sense that his guitar (his axe) will be coin of the realm. But of course the family's instrument of choice isn't the axe but the chainsaw. (In *TCM 2*, Leatherface can't decide whether to set on the female DJ, Stretch, with his saw; he seems to have fallen in love with her. His father, coming on the scene, lays out the cold facts: "You got the choice, boy, sex or the saw; you never know about sex, but the saw, the saw is the family.")

It's not just the guitar remark, by itself a small gesture, that cues you to the film's attitude to the Woodstockers. There's also Franklin. Confined to a wheelchair, Franklin's a whiny, mean, annoying character, who by late in the day has his friends fully exasperated. He's not one of the beautiful people; he's not hip. When the van picks up Hitchhiker, the psychopath, on the side of the road, Franklin connects with him immediately. The other Woodstockers are intrigued by Hitchhiker's tales of the good old days in the slaughterhouse, when they killed the cows with a sledgehammer, up close and personal. But it's Franklin who brings their fascination to the surface. The tales of slaughter and gore create a sort of Bacchic glee in him. His eyes glow and he starts to salivate. Franklin, you might say, is the kids' Gothic id.

One of the most poignant moments in the film comes when Franklin, stuck downstairs in a ruined house (once his grandfather's), unable to move his wheelchair, hears sexual gigglings from the other four upstairs. Trapped and frustrated, Franklin throws back his head and howls like an animal in a trap. (*The* most poignant moment? That's when Leatherface, his nerves badly jangled by all the goings-on of the day, casts himself down in a chair and has a minor nervous breakdown.) Woodstock Nation, ostensibly loving and all inclusive, has no room for the likes of Franklin.

Nor, surely, for Leatherface. But Leatherface and his family, the movie gives us to understand, are what happens when the spirit of Woodstock—Let it all hang out, Be yourself, Do your thing—goes south and penetrates to the dregs. When Franklin lets it all out, you get regression, anger, and confusion. When Leatherface (who, significantly, bears lots of resemblances to Franklin: both are fat, picked-on, inept, mean, scared) lets his spirits flourish, you get mayhem. Maybe the legacy of Crosby, Stills, and Nash and their cohorts ("Hey man, I just gotta say that you people have got to be the strongest bunch of people I ever saw. Three days, man! Three days! We just love you," the band says to the audience in Max Yasgur's fields and in the comfy theater seats for that most audience-flattering of movies, *Woodstock*), maybe the Woodstock legacy is not the Family of Man, but of Manson.

When the kids at Woodstock went into their Rousseau-fed rhapsodies about how humanity was choked by needless, uptight restrictions ("rules and regulations, who needs them? Throw them all away," sing Crosby, Stills, and Nash), what they wanted was more liberty for themselves in a society where Franklin was out of sight and Leatherface didn't exist. No one at Woodstock would have known what to do with Leatherface; but Tobe Hooper, for his part, suggests that Woodstock had a hand in creating him, along with Grandpa, Hitchhiker, Franklin, and Pop.

———————

The inability to face the Gothic antagonist, the spirit that one's own drive for freedom conjures up, arises more than once in

'6os culture. When Ken Kesey writes his grand fable of resistance, *One Flew over the Cuckoo's Nest*, he casts his cartoon superhero, Randall Patrick McMurphy, as a potently dynamic (note the initials, R.P.M.), uncontaminated force. He's pure salutary desire. So is Norman Mailer's hipster, his White Negro, in the essay of that name. So are what Allen Ginsberg, in *Howl*, calls the best minds of his generation, the ones who've been wrecked by oppressive '5os culture: "Destroyed by madness, starving hysterical naked, / dragging themselves through the negro streets at dawn looking for an angry fix."[17] So too are Ntozake Shange's devoted women, in her '6os-inspired play, *For Colored Girls Who Have Considered Suicide When the Rainbow Is Enuf*, who live pure and clean, if poor.

But in no case do these writers wish to contend with the possibility that the forces they most detest may be part of them, or a by-product of their emancipatory visions. Kesey is unwilling to concoct a hero who shares enough qualities with the authoritarian Big Nurse to be drawn to her and thus to make the institutional oppression she represents anything more than a merely external factor. But Big Nurse is only a problem when there's something within a lot of us that seconds her rage for order. McMurphy, to put it in Freud's language, is a man without a superego. That can make him quite appealing, but hardly one of us.

Mailer won't let us make contact with the middle-class Jewish boy who went off to Harvard dressed in all the wrong clothes, and who wants conventional success very much indeed—though he righteously hates that desire, too. Mailer wants us to see him as the pure rebellious stuff, always brave and unbending. His major antagonist is not an attraction to conformity but the fatigue that comes from being an individual, fighting the battle against mediocrity, regimentation, and plastic (the root of all evil, Mailer sometimes seems to think) on behalf of us all. The cruel black men who cruise in and out of the lives of Shange's girls are Gothic monsters, demons whose attractions for the young women never get developed. Why do they need such men? What in them wants relationships that are centrally masochistic?

When Newt Gingrich tries to Gothicize the '60s by saying that Susan Smith's drowning of her children had a source in that all-time permissive decade, he's being foolishly reductive and cynical, but not entirely irrelevant. Our self-idealizations then were dramatic. We often lacked all sense that righteous rebellion against outmoded standards would call up demons—both repressive and regressive—not only from the world of convention and conformity (that was fine; we wanted *that*) but in ourselves and those who would come afterward, too.

The Gothic writers of late-eighteenth-century England knew that the earthshaking events in France would breed hope—"Bliss was it in that dawn to be alive, / But to be young was very Heaven!"—but also intense fears and temptations.[18] Who are we now that prelates and aristocrats have lost their former glory? Angels perhaps, but maybe sadists, too. The general '60s refusal to consider the dark side of its own emancipatory drives resulted in giving that dark side freer rein (as Monk Lewis and Ann Radcliffe could readily have told us it would). To us, it was always Big Nurse who was to blame, or Mailer's shits, or Ginsberg's America. Not us, not us.

When you ask why much of the '60s generation conformed so easily, turned serenely into the boomers, a market segment, one answer isn't very far to seek: we thought that we could never become like the bad ones, thought that we could never get like our parents. Our music, novels, and films had repeatedly told us so—with the result that it was very easy indeed for the pleasure industries to mold us into slightly hipper-looking images of them, playing our music in ads for cars and computers. We'd been to Woodstock (or *Woodstock*), we'd read "The

White Negro," read Kesey—how could we become squares or Big Nurses?

Lionel Trilling famously called the 1960s' cultural rebellion modernism in the streets, but it had far more to do with the movement that's been called Romanticism. The Romanticism of Woodstock was of the Rousseauian, regressive variety; that of Dylan and Hendrix, as I've suggested, has far more in common with Blake's work and its drive to combine pleasure and politics. But modernism, at least in some of its major guises, is, like Rousseauian Romanticism, a revolt against the Gothic, a revolt that continues to smoulder on, even now, in the precincts of high culture. It's a noble revolt, to be sure, far less self-indulgent than the regressive way of Woodstock, and yet hardly more adequate to deal with Gothic energies than the updated ethos of Rousseau proved to be.

To describe modernism's revolt against the Gothic, I'll begin in an odd place, in Jane Austen and her brilliant rebuttal to the Gothic genius of her age. Austen's first novel, probably completed in 1799, but not actually published until 1818, is a parody of Gothic novels in general and of Ann Radcliffe's *Mysteries of Udolpho* in particular. *Northanger Abbey* is the story of Catherine Morland, a rather obtuse and inexperienced young girl, who takes off to Bath for a holiday, chaperoned by a family friend. While at the stylish resort Catherine falls in love with a young man named Henry Tilney. A paragon of male virtue by Austen standards, Tilney is handsome, well-to-do, and commonsensically intelligent, a sort of Doctor Johnson without kinks or tragic depth (without any depth, from what I can see).

Catherine, like everyone else in her set, is an avid reader of Mrs. Radcliffe's novels, especially *Udolpho:* "While I have *Udolpho* to read," she says, "I feel as if nobody could make me miserable."[19] When she's finally invited to visit Henry Tilney's family in their home, Northanger Abbey, she pictures a sublimely dilapidated pile, a vast Gothic tombstone against the blackening sky.

Catherine goes into ecstasies fantasizing over what Northanger will be like. Rhapsodizing to herself about "its long, damp passages, its narrow cells and ruined chapel . . . she could not entirely subdue the hope of some traditional legends, some awful memorials of an injured and ill-fated nun."[20] And for a while, Catherine manages to persuade herself that Henry's father, General Tilney, had in fact done away with his wife, and somewhere in the precincts of the Abbey. But the General, as Catherine is eventually compelled to admit, "is no Montoni." He's simply a callous money-grubber, who, when he discovers that Catherine hasn't much of a fortune to dispense as a dowry for his son, sends her packing. Catherine's fascination with the trappings of lurid Gothic heroines and villains prevented her from identifying a mean-spirited fellow like the General when she met him: she was looking for a more energizing, dramatic kind of evil.

Though written by a young woman in her early twenties, *Northanger Abbey* is a work of remarkable sophistication. It begins with a meditation not just on Catherine Morland per se, but on heroines in novels generally. Throughout the book the narrating voice sustains its awareness—and provokes ours—of the fact that the novel we are reading is an artificial affair, unfolding in a certain relation to preestablished conventions. We're allowed to enjoy Catherine's story as a story, but we're also compelled to recall that it's all being made up, that the characters have as much to do with established literary forms as with people to be met with in life. We meditate on conventions even as we enjoy the pleasures that they bring.

We're encouraged to read self-consciously, though not cynically. And we're also enjoined to measure our ironic way of reading *Northanger* against Catherine's more emotional, self-centered, and un-self-conscious immersion in *Udolpho* (and in life). She longs desperately to be the heroine of a Gothic novel, but it never quite works. When she pries open a great chest of drawers, hoping to find the mandatory charred parchment that will unfold the secret history of the Abbey and offer critical hints about the death of Mrs. Tilney, she discovers only a laundry list. But she keeps on questing, hoping ultimately to find in the blandly self-interested General a Gothic father-ogre to fit her fantasies, and in Northanger Abbey secret passages and exciting hidden places not unlike those concealed in the depths of Udolpho, Otranto, and (perhaps) her own mind.

So we learn, through Austen, to read the Gothic novel as an adolescent indulgence. It's a way to fabricate excitement in a dull life. Avidity for Gothic is also a sign of Catherine's sexual ripeness, which, without a marriage soon, may pass a little beyond ripeness. Gothic beckons to someone like Catherine (and to us), offering what appears to be a shortcut into the secrets of adult life (the General did *it*), a lowest-common-denominator version of sex and power, of what's hidden in the bedroom. But we've got to resist that shortcut, the young Austen insists. Once Gothic has awakened our curiosity, we need to acquire more patient, comprehensive, and subtle tools of analysis, leaving the novels of Mrs. Radcliffe as the mere entertainments that they are (and taking up the civilized, self-conscious work of Jane Austen).

Stanley Cavell suggests that one of the objectives of the modernist work is to investigate its own conditions of possibility. It makes of its artifice a theme, asking the reader to suspend herself between un-self-conscious immersion and total alienation. Modernism as such is a relatively cerebral mode. It solicits a running critical commentary that follows along and intermingles with the traditional tendencies in the work. Reading Austen's novel, one might feel what many have felt about other, more recent modernist works: that it's too chilly; that it goes too far in denying emotion, the uncanny, and the drives. There is no reason, for instance, that a deep immersion in Gothic would not have made Catherine more alert to the likes of General Tilney, more disposed to seeing beneath the surface of his behavior. Hyperbole can incite revelation, too.

If the Gothic mode sometimes goes overboard in exposing the powers of the irrational, one might say that modernism, at least insofar as it's exemplified by Austen's novel, is too squeaky clean. Closer to the present, you see the inadequacy—as well as the acumen—of the modernist mind in Rieff's reflections on Bradshaw and the inner-child movement and Frederick Crews's on recovered memory: both writers, penetrating as they are, can't imagine that there is truth somewhere within the garish excess. And Austen, hypercivilized, brilliantly gifted though she is, really has no idea how one might see books like *Mysteries of Udolpho* or *The Monk* as more than diversions, how one might use them to help provoke certain kinds of revelation.

In the 1990s a revival of Jane Austen began. There have been film versions of *Sense and Sensibility*, of *Pride and Prejudice*, and of *Emma* (as *Clueless*). And of course, it is easy to see resurrected Jane Austen as an antidote to the pressing Gothic energies that are all around. For after *Northanger Abbey*, nothing uncanny mars the world of Austen. You'll find pride, wrath, and most of the other seven deadly sins, but no hauntings, no possessions, nothing that eclipses reason or seriously challenges the conventions by which even her most independent characters tend to regulate their lives. Nineteen-nineties Austen is a refined British holiday away from current Gothic excess.

Oddly enough, a sort of preemptive Gothicizing strike against Jane Austen has come from the academy. Some scholars have been trying to do to her what Freud did to childhood overall: find sexual possession where there was, ostensibly, innocence. Thus Eve Sedgwick's paper "Jane Austen and the Masturbating Girl" and the headline of an issue of *London Review of Books:* "Was Jane Austen Gay?"

In reflecting on the relations between the Gothic and modernism, we shouldn't forget the high priest of high modernism, T. S. Eliot. Eliot's championing of impersonality in the great essay "Tradition and the Individual Talent" can easily be seen as a reaction against the sort of Freudian, Gothic responsiveness to emotion that Eliot associated with irrationalism and the appetite for destruction. Eliot famously disliked *Hamlet,* preferring the authoritarian *Coriolanus* by far. For Eliot the modernist, the Gothic world of *Hamlet* was, I suspect, oppressively overdetermined. Everything in *Hamlet* means too intensely and too much, so that there is no way for the present to draw freely on the past. There's no possibility in such a world, the precursor to the Freudian world in which everything also signifies exhaustively, to freely shore cultural fragments against one's ruin.

More than disliking Hamlet the character, I imagine, Eliot disliked the way that Freud used him as a basis for the Oedipus complex. Eliot, who greatly valued the free play of the mind (of his own mind at least), probably couldn't bear to see literature's most complexly rendered intellectual used to illustrate a theory proclaiming that we were all determined, intellectually and emotionally, by events that had occurred before we had reached full consciousness. Yet to try to banish the Gothic past and Freud—against whom, Katherine Spurlock argues, Eliot implicitly directed a good deal of his cultural criticism—with recourse to a notion like artistic impersonality probably goes too far.[21] To say that creation is a matter of continually extinguishing the personality, turning the mind into a medium, implausibly purges the contingent, the passionate, the uncanny. Going too far to deny the Gothic, Eliot comes up with an untenably idealizing theory of poetry.

The differences within, and the complexities of, modernism are beyond my scope here, but one might fruitfully, if partially, see that movement as a rebellion against the sloppy, emotional (female) excesses that proliferate in the Gothic. The modernism of American painting at mid-century, for example, at least as it was theorized by its major advocates, can be understood as an effort to banish the surface/depth, appearance/reality, ego/id sorts of dichotomies on which Gothic thrives and to render an experience of pure form. Writing in 1949 Clement Greenberg, the most influential art critic of the day, set out to define what he called "our period style." Greenberg described the kind of work of art that then mattered as "an open, more or less transparent object whose effect lies mainly in its total design . . . The interest is in lines of force, thrusts, in the 'activation' of empty space."[22] "The new art style," Greenberg continues, "breathes rationalization." And it is "uninflated by illegitimate content—no religion or mysticism or political certainties."[23] All medium, no message. Greenberg describes an art that you can't read anything into, an art with no unconscious.

If one takes the purging of the Gothic to be a central—though hardly the sole—motive for a good deal of modernist work, then one may see that project most intensely unfolding in the world of architecture. And again, one might, just a little facetiously, give priority to Jane Austen. For the abbey that Catherine Morland finds when she finally makes her visit to the Tilneys is anything but haunted. It has just undergone renovation, and General Tilney is exceedingly proud of being able to show off all its modern conveniences. He's converted Northanger Abbey from a gloomy, old-fashioned Gothic structure to a sparklingly well-lit edifice that's just the place for young Henry's hyperrational disquisitions—directed often to the haplessly ignorant Catherine—on all subjects under the Johnsonian firmament. (She even has to hear an intricate lecture on garden aesthetics.)

Though she doesn't have vast plate-glass windows to deploy—they weren't perfected until the beginning of the twentieth century—Austen the novice architect does all she can to exorcise Northanger Abbey, and in a way that the modernists of more than a hundred years later would approve:

> The furniture was in all the profusion and elegance of modern taste. The fire-place, where [Catherine] had expected the ample width and ponderous carving of former times, was contracted to a Rumford, with slabs of plain though handsome marble, and ornaments over it of the prettiest English china. The windows, to which she looked with peculiar dependence, from having heard the General talk of his preserving them in their Gothic form with reverential care, were yet less what her fancy had portrayed. To be sure, the pointed arch was preserved—the form of them was Gothic—they might be even casements—but every pane was so large, so clear, so light![24]

More light than dark, alas: where is the murky stained glass, the dirt and cobwebs?

More light. The archetypal modernist glass box, the sort of building designed by Mies, Philip Johnson (in his pre-postmodernist phase), or Le Corbusier is, at least in conception, the furthest thing possible from a haunted house. It's radiant with sunlight, a place where nothing uncanny can transpire. The uncanny, which is one of Freud's most common terms for the Gothic, entails the return of the repressed. To Freud, the uncanny is *das Unheimliche,* the unhomelike, but at the same time it is entirely homelike, entirely of the house, in that it is informed by the Oedipal passions that family life always engenders. The modernists (from Austen on?) were out to design houses that, in effect, could never become theaters for the uncanny, never become objective correlatives for the Freudian psyche. Where there were no shadows, no dark spaces, no uncomprehended recesses, there could be no ghosts. So they hoped to give the lie to the Freudian Gothic, to exorcise the house.

Modernism in architecture was devoted to the ethos of transparency. By creating dwellings and offices that had no room for clutter and ornament and that were exclusively functional, you removed the dead hand of the past from contemporary enterprises. You built more cheaply, more efficiently, with homage only to the pragmatic. Citizens would spend less of their time paying for such pared-down dwellings. Workers would be inspired by the no-nonsense, waste-free surroundings to proceed in an aptly expeditious, productive spirit. As the architectural scholar Anthony Vidler observes (not without irony), "If houses were no longer haunted by the weight of tradition and the imbrications of generations of family drama, if no cranny was left for the storage of the bric-a-brac once deposited in damp cellars and musty attics, then memory would be released from its unhealthy preoccupations to live in the present."[25]

The building without cellars or garrets, without hidden rooms, small, aloof chambers, crannies, and crawl spaces was emblematic too of an attitude toward knowledge. What was wanted was clear understanding, unfazed by tricky shifts and hidden meanings, unplumbable depths. In the modernist building, the eye went freely, undeluded, as it might travel when engaged in disinterested scientific inquiry.

Freud had suggested that the psyche was a house, specifically a haunted old Victorian manse. Modernist architects took the cue. We might start by purifying the house, purging it of demons, and so reform the darkened psyche of the present. We might strive to make the inner life resemble the glass structure by Corbu and come to know ourselves with perfect clarity.

The suspension of limits, the cleansing of opacity, signaled a potential lifting of human limits. The eye traveled out into the sky from the glassed-in study or office and saw no end to its dominion. Up high, the head bathed in infinite light and space, the dweller or worker in the glass structure saw all, became all, like the Emersonian transparent eyeball (a strangely modernist image for him).

This sense of world power fit with the theory of self-knowing that the International Style seemed to endorse. The modernist eye could look through room upon room of clear space, could see into everything, overcome borders, walls, repressions, evasions: it could see into the life of things. A knowing that was equated with perfect 20-20 sight; the I as an active, penetrating eye. We could get it right once and for all.

But even in its own architectural terms the International Style presented contradictions. One saw one's own image, vague, spectral (haunting), looking wanly back as one stared out through the great panes of glass. Reflection came on to spoil clarity. And with visual reflection comes self-consciousness, reflection of an intellectual sort. Suddenly the all-seeing self is an interpreter, aware of her particular perspective, the idiosyncratic slant of light that defines and delimits what she sees. And she is also, of course, an object of interpretation. Living in a glass house you probably shouldn't get stoned, for the outsiders, too, can see in. The glass house is a window to the people on the street and to the street people. Like the film screen that projects visions of astounding bourgeois wealth around the world, stirring discontent, sometimes murderous, in the most dismal squats ("Give us Lexuses and Apples and

Now!") the glass wall of Le Corbu displaces the solid wall of the bourgeois domicile, the one that Ibsen temporarily peeled away for his dramas, and puts the life of prosperity on display at all times. One is seen by the wretched: those who have, according to some, turned Manhattan into a third-world city, bums, gangstas, dealers, street prophets, city criers, the mad, Freddy and his ilk: they want in.

The International Style posed itself as a clean break from the past. Thus Corbusier: "If we eliminate from our hearts and minds all dead concepts in regard to the house . . . we shall arrive at the 'House Machine,' the mass-production house, healthy (and morally so too) and beautiful in the same way that the working tools and instruments which accompany our existence are beautiful."[26] Eliminate all dead concepts, old ghosts.

But of course the glass structure was haunted from the start: reflective, vulnerable, the signature for epistemological pride. From the Gothic point of view the glass box is an act of ultimate hubris. It suggests that we no longer need to recall the past. The old manse, crammed with ornament, keepsakes, hand-me-downs, antiques, and curiosities, recalls the weight of past generations. Living amidst their accumulation, the Gothic sensibility affirms, one comprehends how much of life has been scripted in advance. Significant change is understood as entailing the energy—and ruthlessness—that would be involved in moving, throwing away, or rearranging all of these objects. The Victorian domicile shows one how tenacious is the hold of habit, the imprint of character, the force of what has been done over and over, the strength of genes, heredity, biology. The Gothic house affirms what's given over what is wished for.

At the end of his career, the American man of letters, Edmund Wilson, used to repair every summer to his family home, a stone Gothic structure, in upstate New York. Leaving his wife, Elena, and the sunny spaces of Cape Cod, where he spent the rest of the year, Wilson in his last decade went off to meditate on his past and on final things. "Rehearse death," Epictetus, the Stoic philosopher, told his pupils, and Gothic architecture can induce such reflections on mortality. (Radcliffe says at the close of *Udolpho* that the book is addressed particularly to the mourners.) The high modernist in his glass box, deploying his Archimedean gaze, might presume to live forever.

But one doesn't have to marshal vaunting existential reasons here, at least not exclusively. People live in old houses because they like them, because they offer comfort and assurance. The modernists conceived a world of social justice as the corollary to their Utopian housing. But in the presiding Hobbesian war of each against all, some want a comfy bunker to retire to at day's end. Maybe it is a seat of illusions—too smug and cozy a place to reflect the negative truths about human life and its limits—but those illusions can keep one going. Thus a gentle soul like Gaston Bachelard comes along to rehaunt the house in spiritually enlarging ways. Bachelard claimed that he could not dream well—which for him meant making contact with a nourishing unconscious life—in the geometric cube he inhabited in Paris. He needed sheltered, secure spaces that brought back the womb, and the earth at its most hospitable. In *The Poetics of Space* he writes, "If I were asked to name the chief benefit of the house, I should say: the house shelters daydreaming, the house protects the dreamer, the house allows one to dream in peace."[27]

Hard-core Gothicists struck back more violently than the sweet-tempered Bachelard ever could have. As Freud haunts childhood, so Alfred Hitchcock, in his most influential film, struck a blow against modernist hubris. The way we signify our satisfaction with the highway motel we're compelled to stop at on our car trek cross-country is to say that it looks like no one has ever been there, it's so clean. In other words, it has no past. The ranch-style highway motel is a feat of architectural low modernism. But after Hitchcock it is difficult to say of a motel, especially while in the shower, that no one's ever been there. Hitchcock saw that the blank slate of modernist architecture could easily be invaded by the Gothic monster. After *Psycho*, motels are indissociable from loony Norman Bates and the glowering mansion next door (which Hitchcock thought of as one of the stars of the film).

To the degree that modernism is embodied by the anti-Gothic transparent box, to that degree Freud (and Hitchcock, for all purposes Freud's visual secretary) would say that it is bound to fail. For Freud, in his Gothic mode, reserves his greatest scorn for those who believe they have evolved beyond the claims of the instincts, thinking, in the high modernist fashion, that the past is like a library or a museum, a compilation of the best that is known and thought, from which they may freely draw.

Tattoos—which one architectural modernist derided as body ornaments, saying that they were the mark of the killer-to-be, the urban savage—are now all the rage among our Gothic, tribal young. They wear Poe-esque brands, indelible marks of the intention (or hope) to sin. And they come decked out in chains, their bodies variously pierced to signify limit, capture, enclosure, or perhaps their awareness that the drives are in command and that the erogenous zones—preferred sites for piercing—hold one in Gothic thrall. The kids look like stylized dungeon escapees, which is pretty much the point. Those who've been well pierced and tattooed are hardly ready for life in the glass box—post-apocalyptic primitives, they inhabit an urban jungle—or will find much revelation in "Tradition and the Individual Talent" or *Sense and Sensibility*.

Whatever the nobility of the modernist tradition that runs from Austen to T. S. Eliot and beyond, it stood little chance against its Gothic antagonist. Too often modernism was obsessively, programmatically cleansing: no hint of messy unreason—nothing female (as it was then understood to be)—ought to survive. As exhilarating as some of the best modernist work is intellectually, it often succeeds ill as art in that it purges too much from experience in order to achieve its intensities. (Note that however modernist Eliot the critic might be, especially in policy papers like "The Function of Criticism," he knows how to trap darker, more disturbing energies in his poems.) Modernism defeats the Gothic too completely and so allows for its return and eventual triumph.

Literary modernism, despite a few academics still poring over their Pound and Eliot, is a stuffed bird on taxidermist Norman Bates's shelf. But the modernist impulse (or *a* modernist impulse)—let's clean it up, whatever it is; purify and intellectualize at all costs—still has a place in American cultural life. The desire for a clean, clear window on the world informs much of our political discourse, economic projection, analytical philosophy, and legal thinking. By utterly denying the Gothic, and especially messy Gothic passions, these intellectual forms have put themselves out of touch with large dimensions of human experience. Part of what makes us now susceptible to the Gothic world-view, I suspect, is the failure of modernism to provide a plausible alternative to the Gothic mode, a perspective that could actually include the Gothic without submitting entirely to it. And easy Romanticism, Gothic's main contemporary alternative in current culture, is, even at its best, too thin, too much a form of spiritual travel literature to offer much cogent opposition.

But what we have learned from our survey of turn-of-the-century modernism and current and '60s ersatz Romanticism remains of value. For we have seen that Gothic can indeed be challenged, nobly or foolishly. And such a challenge might be carried on with more brio, more acumen and intensity. In fact Gothic does have a major cultural antagonist, an antagonist that is also an ally, though that fact has been hidden from most of us for some time. To describe that counterforce, I need to take a crooked path through a number of diverse figures and phenomena, from Freud to Sylvester Stallone, from Percy Bysshe Shelley to Toni Morrison.

S & M
CULTURE

What happens if the culture of Gothic goes uncontested? What if its influence grows, it becomes sharper, more subtle, more pervasive, and what if nothing comes along to counter the Gothic drive?

To answer this question we need not look far, for Freud in fact wrote a book that describes an internal culture in which Gothic triumphs, in which there is nothing of consequence to oppose to the spirit of Edgar Allan Poe. On the last page of *Civilization and Its Discontents,* Freud, having given us a vision of a fully haunted psyche, announces that perhaps the eternal spirit of Eros will come along to challenge the spirits of Death and Necessity now apparently in command. But Freud, great Gothic mythmaker though he is, cannot imagine what that contemporary Eros would be like. That he leaves for others. And, as our reflections on Forrest Gump, Iron John, and all the rest have shown, we have not succeeded at all well in meeting Freud's challenge. Our culture seems largely without a persuasive counterforce to its Gothic drives. My objective in this chapter is to point the way to a more potent version of Gothic-battling Eros than either Freud or Robert Bly succeeds in conceiving.

Earlier I described Freud's internalizing of the Gothic. He brought the haunted castle inside, called it the psyche, and populated it with ghosts—or rather, in the Freudian parlance, imagoes, figments of highly invested figures from the past. "At first," says J. H. van den Berg, "only the parents, who could not stand being outside any longer, required shelter, finally it was the entire ancestry."[1] In Freud's early work, from the 1900 *Interpretation of Dreams* to the 1914 "On Narcissism," the castle was, as it were, haunted from below. The monsters lived in the suppressed, subterranean regions of the self, within the unconscious. Appropriately for Gothic, it was at night, when we dreamed, that the spirits purportedly walked.

But in 1930 Freud confirms a new vision of the haunted psyche. The psyche now is haunted not just from below but also from above. In *Civilization and Its Discontents,* Freud conceives the most brilliant and influential version of the Gothic hero-villain that we currently possess. He shows us—or rather he allows us to see—where an uncontested Gothic drive might lead.

Civilization and Its Discontents famously reflects on the conflict between the demands of civilization and the claims of the instincts. The Freudian subject is possessed by a variety of intense, often unconscious needs, needs for sexual satisfaction and for the release of aggression. On the other side is civilization, inhibiting the drives. Though it takes its toll in frustration, civilization also prevents us from committing—and from being victims of—murder, rape, and incest. In *Civilization and Its Discontents* Freud describes the conflict between the passions and the law in starker, more original and dramatic terms than he, or perhaps anyone, had done before, leaving us with an uncompromisingly bleak and persuasively Gothic vision of Western humanity's state.

In one sense at least—in Hegel's—the book is a Gothic tragedy, one that takes the entire world for its stage. In Hegel's view, which bases itself in *Antigone,* much as Aristotle's does in *Oedipus Rex,* it is the contention between consequential but competing goods that is at the root of tragedy. The first right that Freud champions in *Civilization and Its Discontents* is the right of our instincts. From early on in his career Freud had been desire's advocate. Not that he wanted all appetites let loose on the world, but he did want the primary instincts to be acknowledged and respected.

Yet there is a second right in *Civilization and Its Discontents,* and Freud feels as much allegiance to it as he does to the *it*'s domain, the unconscious, which after all he claimed to have been the first to understand scientifically. (The poets, Freud acknowledged, often traveled through the territory of the unconscious, but they couldn't draw an accurate map of it after they'd emerged.) The second right is of course civilization itself.

Freud's view that there is a deep-rooted conflict between society and the individual is hardly original with him: the idea was a commonplace among the so-called Romantic writers. Part of Freud's originality lies in his arguing that civilization isn't just an external phenomenon. Rather it exists within us, an active, influential element that is a part of the self. The superego, civilization's internal agent, watches over us from inside, "like a garrison in a conquered city." Unlike the Rousseauian poet, who tends to believe that he and his like-minded friends can set themselves up in thorough opposition to an unjust social order, Freud believes that even the most rebellious of us contain the principle of oppression—the principle that we most detest—as a major element in our self-identities. The I that would oppose society already *is* society right to its core.

And the superego treats us unjustly, asking us to renounce too much. It's not only sex that civilization restricts; the more pressing problem is that of aggression. With the advent of civilization, what happened to the aggression that we all contain, that comes hard-wired into homo sapiens to preserve the species? Surely that violence couldn't be directly expressed; it would destroy civilized life with a war of each against all.

To Freud, aggressive energy, the outward expression of which is prohibited by civilization, turns inward. It becomes the property of the interior agent of conscience, the superego, and is used to punish our purportedly immoral desires. Freud puts matters succinctly: "The effect of instinctual renunciation on the conscience then is that every piece of aggression whose satisfaction the subject gives up is taken over by the super-ego and increases the latter's aggressiveness (against the ego)."[2]

But Freud pushes his argument further: the superego, he observes, punishes us not only for the transgressions we commit, but also for those that we merely conceive. Because the superego is, as Freud asserts, "omniscient," nothing gets by it. And since the superego is at least partly unconscious, the whole dynamic of desire and punishment can go on outside our awareness.

The Gothic dimension of this work may now be apparent. In *Civilization and Its Discontents,* the psyche begins to look like a sadomasochistic dungeon, with the cruel superego tormenting the hapless ego. What we often feel day to day are the results of the endless lashings that the superego (the "over-I," to translate the German literally) administers to the dependent self. Those results include fatigue, depression, lack of interest in sex, in new experiences, in life. At its worst, the over-I can become so ferocious in its unfounded enmity against the I—so full of frustrated aggression—that it drives the individual to suicide. The superego, says Freud in a sorrowful line, can create a pure culture of death in the psyche.

What makes the superego a Gothic hero-villain? The fact that we are damned with it and without it; the fact that, like Montoni, like Ambrosio, like O. J. Simpson in his media renderings, the superego is both depraved and emblematic of elevated values. For it represents civilization. Without it, social strife would unfold nakedly and with horrific results; the barbarians would beat down the gates and they would be ourselves. Yet with the superego we are condemned to a life of self-torture, and of course to mistreating others when they become surrogates for our own hapless egos. We may detest Freud's Gothic hero-villain, but we probably do not want to do away with it entirely.

How shall we describe the relationship between Freud's superego and the ego that it tortures for its pleasure, giving that ego a sense of security, a sense of identity, at the expense of ever-increasing pain? The answer should be clear enough from the terms of the question, though we arrive here at a formulation that Freud resisted making: the relation between the ego and the superego, in Freud's Gothic psyche, is sadomasochistic. The major agencies take their pleasure from inflicting pain and from experiencing it.

The id, the focus of Freud's reflections in the early work, is correspondingly diminished in import in *Civilization and Its Discontents:* it's the source of the over-I's energy; it's the I's antagonist; but its status as purely desiring agency seems now to matter little. Desire, and love, are leaving the picture. Guilt and punishment, both experienced ambivalently, both experienced as pleasure-pain, are the order of the day. Freud, in *Civilization and Its Discontents*, is right on the verge of saying that, for all purposes, in our culture our interior lives have become sadomasochistic systems, and that they will become more intensely so as time goes on. For Freud, to be sadomasochistic is to be normal; we're all sadomasochists.

Writing of sadomasochism, Michel Foucault observes that it "is not a name given to a practice as old as Eros; it is a massive cultural fact which appeared precisely at the end of the eighteenth century, and which constitutes one of the great conversions of Western imagination."[3] In general, one ought to be cautious about subscribing too quickly to Foucault's historical generalizations. It was Foucault, after all, who claimed that the ship of fools—a boat loaded with the city's madmen and -women and set adrift—was a historical actuality, not the literary device it was. And yet on the matter of sadomasochism and history, Foucault does seem to be on to something. Some of the Roman emperors, as described by Tacitus and Suetonius, take an obviously sexual delight in their cruelty; Italian Renaissance depictions of the saints in their martyrdom fluently conjoin eros and torment; a plate from Hogarth's *Harlot's Progress* (1731) shows birch rods decorating the bedroom of the prostitute (in Gillray's prints, such devices are put directly to use); one could add endlessly to such a list. But the obsessive conjunction of sex with cruelty in Western literature and visual art does seem to explode with Foucault's hero, Sade, and with the Revolution.

What relation is there between sadomasochism and the Gothic, beyond the fact that they both take off at the same time and, perhaps, in reaction to some of the same events? It seems to me that sadomasochism is Ur-Gothic, Gothic without elaboration. Many critics have remarked on the conventional nature of the Gothic: Eve Sedgwick, as I noted, observes that no comparably influential literary form is so pervasively a matter of conventions. Of the many topoi that Sedgwick names—doubles, incest, rebellion, and all the rest—three elements seem central. You cannot have Gothic without a cruel hero-villain; without a cringing victim; and without a terrible place, some locale, hidden from public view, in which the drama can unfold.

And these are also the critical elements of sadomasochism. In Freud, the hero-villain is the superego, the heroine the ego, and the terrible inaccessible place the psyche. In external, or interpersonal, sadomasochism, all the drama, or play, takes place in the hidden bedroom or the mock dungeon; there is the sadist, the top; and the masochist, the bottom. It's Castle Udolpho, Montoni, and Emily, all together, without inhibition, evasion, or elaboration—and without hope of deliverance. No rescuer is on the way. Not for nothing were *The Monk* and *Udolpho* among the Divine Marquis' favorite reading.

My view, controversial as it may be, is that in a culture that is in many ways dominated by Gothic, the sadomasochistic mode, in love and in all other human relations as well, will come progressively further to the fore. For S & M is Gothic uncontested by an effective alternative drive; S & M is where Gothic, in a certain sense, wants to go.

A culture approaching pure S & M Gothic would be one where human relations, especially erotic relations, would always be defined as power relations. Equality in love, as well as in politics and social life generally, would no longer be a tenable ideal. It would be impossible in such a culture to conceive of any relation, with husband, with child, with neighbor, or with friend, except in terms of domination and submission; in an S & M culture, love (if one could still use that word) would always be love of power.

What would bring us to such a point, it is worth emphasizing, would be the proliferation and intensification of the Gothic vision—*without any cogent cultural opposition*. Freud's work is, in effect, a great Gothic novel about Western culture and the individuals who inhabit it. In *Civilization and Its Discontents,* he shows us where the culture he describes is tending—into internal sadomasochism, and perhaps into external forms, too.

And what are we to do? On the last page of the book, Freud says that Eros may now assert himself against his immortal adversary, Death (that is, sadomasochism). But Freud has no idea what that alternative to the Gothic might look like—he lacks a strong myth of love.

Have we reached the culture of S & M that Freud prophesies? Of course not. There are plenty of forces alive that are more vital than those worshipped by death-delighting Poe. And yet, as the millennium draws closer, hard-core Gothic does seem to be enriching its powers.

There is, first off, some superficial evidence that sadomasochism is coming more and more to the cultural forefront. *New York Magazine,* which cannot always be wrong, has proclaimed sadomasochism the sexual mode of the '90s.[4] One thinks of other literal, and immediately recognized, versions of

S & M such as Madonna's pornocopia, *Sex,* with its photos of the material madame in potent and submissive postures, and the notorious "Express Yourself" video that shook up Ted Koppel so. Gianni Versace dressed Cindy Crawford in heavy leather and sent her down the runway, setting a trend soon followed by Betsey Johnson and Thierry Mugler. There's the vogue for piercing and tattoos ("Did it hurt getting that?" has become young America's pick-up line). In *Pulp Fiction* Bruce Willis and Ving Rhames find themselves in the hands of some good old boys who're deep into hard-core S & M; it's an updated, urban reprise of *Deliverance's* most memorable scene. Robert Mapplethorpe has become, in the eyes of many, a consequential artist.

But these matters are epiphenomenal, froth on the top of the glass. What Freud helps us to see is how the Gothic phenomena we have described in the book so far tend toward the sadomasochistic plot. That the sadomasochistic psyche may be becoming the order of the day (somewhat as Christopher Lasch said that the narcissistic psyche was the order of the 1970s) is suggested simply by the proliferation of Gothic that we have been taking note of. For the common content in much of the work we have considered, from Radcliffe to Rice, consists of more or less sublimated versions of the sadomasochistic encounter.

Our collective pleasure in contemplating O. J., Michael Jackson, Freddy Krueger, the satanic ritual scandals, Oprah's guests, the victims of abuse, Gothic TV and all the rest may here find further explanation. We are drawn to such things, Freud's elaborated line of thinking would run, because they reflect a pervasive interior state: they reflect the sadomasochistic tendencies in our own psyches. To put matters crudely, we take pleasure in identifying our pleasures with those of the Gothic hero-villain, the sadist; we take pleasure in becoming, in fantasy, the Gothic victim, the heroine. In a sense, all of the

Gothic examples that I have elaborated in the book, from *Silence of the Lambs* to Anne Rice to high theory, might be taken as proof that Freud is, if not right point for point, at least ahead of us in his conception of where our own culture might be going.

For at the core of every Gothic plot is the S & M scenario: victim, victimizer, terrible place, torment. From the psychoanalytical point of view, all of Gothic literature and film could be seen as the effort to purvey—while disguising, for the benefit of censors, internal and external—the pleasures of the sadomasochistic encounter.

———

In the world that Freud prophesies, and that we now see stirrings of, sadomasochism would be the normal state of the psyche. Sadomasochistic sex would be normal sex.

And I mean compulsively sadomasochistic sex, not the currently fashionable theatrical version. In a culture of pure Gothic, a culture of Poe, no one would be able to conceive of pleasure outside the circuit of domination and surrender. There would be no conception of love, no room to wish for the happiness of others, for their pleasure, their growth into imaginative prowess and complexity of character. Rendered cynical by the Gothic, dead-end and no-fault, we would not be able to believe that such love is tenable. Freud, a humane man, deeply wanted to affirm such a love at the close of *Civilization and Its Discontents*, but though he could manage to believe in its possibility, he couldn't conceive its form. Without that love, the sadomasochistic way, in which Gothic is reduced to its basic terms, will, I suspect, grow stronger.

At present, many members of the gay community, and more and more straights, are becoming involved in consensual sadomasochism. Consensual sadomasochistic sex is generally not akin to felonious assault or rape. Most S & M relationships are not only consensual, but contractual. The top and the bottom, the sadist and the masochist, enter into a complex agreement about what sorts of punishment will be inflicted: how tightly the thongs are to be secured; how the whip will be deployed; what use is to be made of handcuffs, hoods, gags, blindfolds, cock rings, tit clamps, paddles, riding crops, and the rest; where the boundaries of chastisement and humiliation stand. A range of signals issued by the bottom, who in many ways controls the encounter, determines where the torment desists.

In the economy of sadomasochistic sex, it's been said, pleasure and guilt enter into a satisfying reciprocal relationship. For the masochist, pleasure is paid for immediately and fully with pain. The masochist can enjoy piquant, long-wished-for joys that conscience has forbidden, for now conscience can also have what it deeply desires: the pleasure of punishing the transgressions. Morality and appetite are alternately satisfied. (It's as though a composer had scored a perfectly balanced duet for two implacable divas.) The masochist, we're told, often leaves the encounter in a state of harmony, moral and sexual passions both expended, the inner balance at soothing zero. As to the sadist, he or she can purportedly express and, in expressing, discharge the ferocity of the superego. For the sadist, S & M would involve a purging, a catharsis.

Explanations for the practice are multiple, but many participants contend that they are gaining some mastery over their previously unconscious drives for domination and submission by playing them out in a controlled, theatrical environment. They are, in effect, out ahead of the S & M curve. For if indeed we are evolving into S & M psyches, if pleasure must always be, in today's culture, pleasure-power, then it is better to know as much, and to pay proper respects to the power drive by integrating it self-consciously into sex. Then one can perhaps play with the drive for cruelty, rather than being its unwitting object, the dark king's pawn. Consensual

S & M, perhaps, makes the best of a bad situation. If our psyches have gone—or are going—over to Gothic, why not own to the fact and both indulge in and limit our hunger for domination and submission?

Perhaps. But I tend to concur with Leo Bersani when he observes that one is doing little to modify standing modes of oppression simply by placing the oppressed—the gay man, say—on the top and letting him, somewhat playfully, lord it over a willing bottom.[5] Then too, it is not clear for how long S & M remains a game, stays ironic. At what point does role-playing disappear and obsession take over? For very few is an urbane irony compatible with sexual ardor. I expect that often what begins in sophisticated farce ends in an intensity and maybe too a passion that is closer to the tragic.

For in a culture of Gothic—and an S & M encounter may just be a very compressed Gothic culture—there is no love to mitigate the drive to domination, not even a conception of love that can adequately counter the Gothic myth that all is haunted and that death inevitably wins out. In the life of the psyche and in intense relations between persons, sadomasochism will, Freud suggests, be the order of the day. But what might our more public and general life be under the reign of Poe? Where does Gothic take us in social terms? And how, my central question remains, might we counter such a fate?

In 1985, Sylvester Stallone starred in a film inelegantly titled *Rambo: First Blood, Part 2,* a production that, however crude, may have more than a little to teach about the dynamics of contemporary *social* sadomasochism. The film came out during the period when Stallone was Hollywood's all-in-all; when Rocky and Rambo seemed to have caught and embodied some significant quotient of America's spirit. *First Blood* enacts an absorbing reversal. In it, John Rambo, Vietnam veteran, goes back to Vietnam to free abandoned U.S. POWs, and in effect does to the Russian troops who're in the country, along with their Vietnamese allies, something like what the Viet Cong did to us Americans during the war.

Looking like a comic book battle-hero, with bandanna, leonine mane, pumped biceps and pecs, Rambo uses all sorts of guerilla stunts—he buries himself in a mud bank; he flourishes a bow and arrows, with and without explosive tips—to foil the communists. Fast-moving, lightly armed, ruthless, he hits and runs free time and again. The Russians play the role that in actuality often belonged to us beleaguered Americans. Vietnam redeemed.

But then Rambo gets captured, and the central scene begins. It's a torture scene. Grabbed by the Russians, Rambo is bound up, in near-cruciform no less, to take what they can dish out. And this he does, with massive courage. In fact he does it with a passionate intensity that borders on pleasure. Rambo is energized by being able to take it, to show what a man he is; but there's also an ardor in his face that is perceptibly erotic. The electric shocks have something of an orgasmic effect (as well as doing amazing things for his upper body definition).

Why is it a pleasure to see Rambo tortured? Why are we willing to *pay* for this sort of thing? For something like the reason that people found it pleasing to see Sylvester Stallone take violent beatings in the *Rocky* movies (at least after they'd watched the first one and gotten the hang of the plots): because you know that Stallone is going to pay the enemy back tenfold. And the further the enemy goes in torturing him, the more brutal, cruel, and crazy they are, the further Stallone can go in taking his revenge. The more outrageous the torture, the more violence we'll be able to enjoy with a clean conscience. Because, Hollywood knows, violent revenge is OK if the crime being answered is heinous enough. (In the development of this film conceit, Sam Peckinpah is the all-time genius; *Straw Dogs* perhaps the mainstream apogee.) So, crucified on a rusted old box spring, John Rambo faces humiliation, electric shock, and burns, until finally he can shed his bonds and wreak havoc on the assembled company—though not before picking up the radio and informing the corrupt Americans at home base that he's coming after them. It's payback time.

And for payback time to work, Rambo has to take a lot; the Russians have to go way into debt. In fact Rambo even seems to savor his pain because he knows what's coming. The pleasure circuit in this film runs from masochism to sadism, from pain to payback.

Does this seem like an isolated instance? Think for a moment: how much of our national cinema—our national dream life, perhaps—is obsessed with the revenge plot, which is to say with some version, however displaced, of the masochism-sadism circuit? (Under the rubric of Revenge, the comprehensive *Video Hound's Golden Movie Retriever* lists well over a thousand titles.) Think of the grand revenge sequences at the end of the *Godfather* films (our national epics of retribution). The image of Corleone foe Moe Greene getting plugged through the lens of his glasses, while lying on a massage table somewhere in Las Vegas, sticks indelibly with the viewer. Clint Eastwood has often played the role of the archetypal American revenger, but you've got to humiliate him first. Humiliate him, then die, like the desperados he pops from the fence one by one, musical notes played off their stave by a virtuoso.

There are, I think, fewer revenge films around now than in the wake of Vietnam, though it's hard to imagine cinema without images of the great comeback, the grand overthrow of the rotten powers by our once-humbled heroes. (The top of sports pleasure, for many, is the come-from-behind win, and the triumphal yap of the victorious underdog. How many watch hyperkinetic games like football and basketball to savor the comebacks, seeing their own imagined triumph after humiliation played out?)

But if you'll think back to some of the Gothic events, true life and otherwise, that have recently obsessed the nation, you'll see that they also often entail revenge plots: O. J. (in theory) goes after Nicole for fooling around; Lorena snips John for beating her; the Menendez kids take vengeance after years of purported abuse; the drunken wife-beater finally gets his comeuppance from the Oprah audience; Tonya gets back at Nancy, then Nancy at Tonya. There's also Michael Jackson, Timothy McVeigh, Susan Smith: American Gothic often ends in litigation, preferably in public trials where a form of justice, often indistinguishable from collective revenge, gets administered. Crime and punishment and entertainment for all.

Is this a male thing, this fixation with payback? In its most emphatic form, yes. But there is also a female revenge film, the soft-core *Pretty in Pink*—type movie where the heroine plays a plain, poor, socially maligned girl who survives every snub with graces intact and goes on to popularity, finding true love with the ostensibly conceited boy who turns out to be, mirabile dictu, more shy and misunderstood than stuck-up.

Carrie, as written by Stephen King and then put on screen by Brian de Palma, is a boy's raucous translation of that girl's story. Carrie is the high-school outcast, submitted to choral invective from the girls in the shower room when she has her first period ("Plug it up! Plug it up!"); ranked out, maligned, finally elected school prom queen in a burst of guilty benevolence by the other kids, only to be doused with pig's blood on the stage. Then it's day of the locusts. Carrie, who's developed telekinetic powers, executes her payback in macho style by destroying her high school, killing nearly everyone there in a gross conflagration, and taking out most of the town, too: *Rambo* meets *Pretty in Pink*.

I pick *Rambo,* set largely in Vietnam, as a prototypical revenge film because it seems that in the wake of our defeat in Southeast Asia the popular hunger for such films intensified. Having lost the war, we needed to take back the high ground, to see our innocent stand-ins (for what was Rambo but a cartoon image of America?) hurt and humbled, made into the butt, then be resurrected as from the dead (Stallone's films are full of Christological kitsch, crucifixions and pietàs) to dispense rough justice.

When we entered the war in the Persian Gulf, George Bush talked repeatedly about kicking the Vietnam syndrome: a suitably modern Gothic formulation, which suggests that the spirit of revenge is inseparable from the desire to change the meaning of the past, to make it different from what it was. Such an impulse—Nietzsche called it the will's hatred of time and its "it was"—lives a general life and may even help shape such major acts in America as going to war.[6] If we can perfectly offset a past trauma with a symmetrical event in the present, then that disturbing past event in effect never happened: we have a clean slate. It's not so much a matter of evening the score, as people like to put it, as of bringing things back to zero. We want to start the game all over again. (In every revenge scenario, there lies a rebirth fantasy.) I would suggest, then, that if the interior state to which Gothic tends is the sadomasochistic psyche that Freud describes, then the social and political situation in which Gothic reigns triumphant is characterized by the pervasiveness of rancor and revenge.

America's self-conception as being once upon a time primordially innocent may make this fantasy of the clean slate all the more enticing. Never mind that the past trauma *determines* the form of the later redemption, that defeat in Vietnam helped to shove us into the Persian Gulf War, so that we continued to be tied to the past. In other words, we become more Gothic in orientation with our desire to overcome the Gothic predicament, bondage to the past.

Am I stretching the category of sadomasochism too far by associating it with suffering (often of the self-imposed variety) and retribution, revenge? For sadomasochism per se has an overtly sexual element. The same thing cannot be said of revenge. Or can it? For the object of revenge, at least in compulsive vengefulness, almost invariably takes on the attributes of a sexual object: it is intensely contemplated, singled out, fetishized, becoming the center of fantasy and desire. It becomes, as does the object of romantic love, the only thing that exists in the world. In the actual act of revenge there is—or there is imagined to be—a consummation that changes everything, just as erotic consummation is purported to do.

Revenge always involves some kind of repetition. The cycle wheels on, from trauma to purported triumph, assault to vengeance. It's virtually always payback time in America and in the American psyche.

But the external sadomasochistic cycle has much more practical and mundane associations than those I have been describing. Pragmatic psychologists sometimes refer to low-key, day-to-day styles of masochism as stamp-saving. Stamp-saving is the process of storing up grievances, husbanding injuries, slights, insults, becoming, in short, a banker of resentments, then letting that resentment out in one grandly destructive burst. "I've taken all I can from you. I can't stand it any more!" And then payback begins in earnest, maybe not quite as flamboyantly as Rambo executes it, but fiercely enough.

One could do worse than to perform the thought experiment of seeing one's life from the vantage of revenge. How much do we do—have we done—to change what cannot be changed, the past? The most common target of revenge, at least in bourgeois American culture, tends to be one's parents.

A sad pall comes over a classroom when I ask students how many of them have taken up this or that path, a major, a sport, a social life, to show their parents that they were all wrong? How many of them turned away from some sphere they loved to prove themselves elsewhere? These are banal and nonheroic questions, and the answers they induce are not the stuff of high visionary drama: but such questions can often get the center of the day-to-day lives we lead, and so are not to be despised.

Now, cut back in time from Sylvester Stallone's Rambo/America, crucified and tortured, bound to the mattress springs by his Russian captors, and from our own culture of rancor, however large it may be, to Percy Bysshe Shelley's Prometheus, similarly bound and tortured by an arch-foe. The emblem for oppression in Shelley's *Prometheus Unbound,* which I take to be the greatest poem to arise from the visionary movement in late-eighteenth-century England, is the Jupiter who chains Prometheus to the rocks and sends off a vulture every day to feed on the hero's liver. In its insights into the culture of sadomasochism, revenge, and the Gothic, *Prometheus Unbound* remains, I believe, well out ahead of us. We still aren't Shelley's contemporaries.

For Shelley not only teaches the centrality of the sadomasochistic impulse for the post-revolutionary Western self, he also dramatizes a way of breaking out of the compulsively repeated cycle of suffering and perpetrating pain, of bottom and top, slave and master. He engages Gothic to find a way out of Gothic.

Jupiter is a tyrant, as hateful to Shelley as the priggish Russians and Vietnamese who torment John Rambo are to his audience, though the motives for Shelley's enmity are a little more substantial and complex. To Shelley, Jupiter represents, among other things, the worst of the English king and the

Judaeo-Christian God. He's a bitter lord of limits, Jupiter, who takes pleasure in keeping his subjects in a state of protracted dependency. He's a father who makes sure his children never grow up.

The author of *Civilization and Its Discontents* would call Jupiter a sick superego. He'd understand Shelley's association of the basely high-minded god with needless restriction and torture, and with the prohibitive Yahweh. Freud would be less compelled by the political dimension that Shelley adds to his allegory; he had little faith in politics as a sphere for redemption, or even serious improvement. And yet as someone who watched the rise of Nazism and eventually fled to England to avoid persecution, he would understand, at least in some measure, how a thug like Jupiter could get himself elevated to godly status through people's need for security, and for punishment.

There may be no purer manifestation of the spirit of revenge in all history than Freud's arch-foe, the onetime housepainter and perpetual clown who dedicated himself to redeeming Germany's humiliations. The focus of his revenge was, of course, a staple of Gothic literature, the wandering Jew, without home or true allegiance to nation or soil. One might say that Hitler and his countrymen wrote the most horrific Gothic novel of all time.

But what Freud would merely call an ego, an entity that (at least according to the formulations of 1914 and after) is narcissistic in its essence and, even at its healthiest, longs chiefly to protract pleasure and avoid pain, Shelley calls Prometheus. What is the difference?

To Shelley, men and women ought to expect to do more than to live equably, ironically, and sanely, as Freud, in general, teaches we should. We're more than just egos bound to negotiate between the pleasure and reality principles until our races are run. At our best we're the ones who steal fire, the primal powers of nature, and with them create civilizations:

"Cities . . . / Were built," says Shelley of the days before Prometheus's bondage, "and through their snow-like columns flowed / The warm winds, and the azure aether shone / And the blue sea and the shadowy hills were seen."[7] Prometheus is humankind as creator, not only in the arts, but also in the sciences. For Shelley loved science (experiments set his Oxford rooms on fire more than once) and saw little substantial difference between the poet and the inventor devoted to improving humanity's lot.

In *Civilization and Its Discontents* Freud speculates that gaining control over fire was reserved for the primitive man who could restrain himself from pissing the flames out. In what may be his most outrageous footnote—and that is no small distinction; the notes are often where Freud's Shakespearean fool cavorts at the expense of the monarch who's in charge up top—Freud conjectures that the sight of phallic-shaped flames aroused primal men homosexually and made them competitive ("we'll see whose is bigger!"). The resulting event, Freud calmly observes, "was therefore a kind of sexual act with a male, an enjoyment of sexual potency in a homosexual competition."[8]

By controlling the heat of his own sexual enthusiasm, some primal man became the first to gain control over flames. Freud's Prometheus, conqueror of fire, is the man who can regulate his bladder and staunch his homosexual tastes. This Prometheus is a man of renunciation. The first move in creating Freudian civilization is a ludicrous and self-negating gesture, a token of things to come. Shelley's Prometheus preserves vital intensity even as he creates a higher collective and personal life. For Shelley, invention, scientific and aesthetic, has all the fervor of sex, and is corroborated, and even enjoined, by a life of erotic enjoyment.

Shelley's poem—which would dramatize both the workings of an individual mind and the broadly political, hence collective dynamics of lordship and bondage—begins with Prometheus savoring his pain. He's hit the bottom floor of masochistic bliss. "Ah me!" he intones twice, "alas, pain ever, for ever." Prometheus sounds like an impassioned opera star lamenting and reveling in her grief. So Coleridge's Ancient Mariner, whom Camille Paglia calls literature's most influential male heroine, intones his impassioned refrain: "Alone, alone, all, all alone, / Alone on a wide wide sea! / And never a saint took pity on / My soul in agony."[9] The Mariner traverses the world telling his tale over and over, gripped by a compulsion to repeat.

Repetition-compulsion is an ultimate dead-end Gothic state in that it represents the complete triumph of past traumas over future possibility. In *Beyond the Pleasure Principle*, Freud famously associates the compulsion to repeat with the death drive, an organism's urge to return to an earlier state of inorganic life, evolution in reverse gear. The Mariner, in many ways like his creator Coleridge, can't find a way to move beyond past woundings and acquire the power to begin anew. (Coleridge is the most haunted of all the visionary poets.) But Shelley, through his Prometheus, conceives freedom from the Gothic bind, though how plausible that freedom proves will be a major question.

Not long after his wail of masochistic pleasure-pain, Prometheus begins to stoke up fantasies of revenge. A certain sort of victim (me, you, all of us?), Shelley suggests, wants most to be victimizer; the whimpering son hungers to become punitive father. So Prometheus goes into a prospective sadist's rhapsody about what he's going to do to Jupiter when the tyrant's time comes (as an oracle has guaranteed it will):

> And yet to me welcome is day and night,
> Whether one breaks the hoar frost of the morn,
> Or starry, dim, and slow, the other climbs

The leaden-coloured east; for then they lead
The wingless, crawling hours, one among whom
—As some dark Priest hales the reluctant victim
Shall drag thee, cruel King, to kiss the blood
From these pale feet, which then might trample thee
If they disdained not such a prostrate slave.
Disdain! Ah no! I pity thee.[10]

The shift from disdain to pity is rapid, too quick to be credible to some. But to me the velocity of the change suggests that Shelley has driven himself as far as he can in embracing an ethos of revenge, the desire to expunge past humiliations by reversing them in the present, and becoming, in effect, the superego to his superego.

Harold Bloom remarks of Shakespeare's characters that they are the first in literature who overhear themselves speaking, interpret what they've said, and so garner the power to change. (They strongly misread not others but themselves, to use Bloom's idiosyncratic terms.) However persuasive Bloom's idea is about Shakespeare, it applies quite aptly to Shelley in *Prometheus Unbound*.

Note how Prometheus overhears, then reconsiders his own key word, redolent with sadistic loathing, "disdain": "[T]hese pale feet, which then might trample thee / If they *disdained* not such a prostrate slave. / *Disdain!* Ah no! I pity thee." It takes considerable power, intellectual and moral, to both express one's own obsessions in the most eloquently passionate language, and to take up a critical, a listening, position.

Prometheus is both patient and analyst to himself. Freud believed that the only way to sustain a free flow of thoughts in analysis is to let go completely, to free-associate. The patient flows, the analyst listens critically, intervening when need be. One self is divided between two personages, with the analyst playing the role of receptive, interpreting mind. Yet as even

Freud admitted, such a strategy of self-excavation gives rise to a master-slave dynamic; he calls it the transference. For the patient almost always ends up resenting the analyst's interpretive power and casting the doctor as an authoritarian foe. Then the S & M cycle begins again and becomes the subject of analysis. Shelley would, I suspect, have been sympathetic to Karl Kraus's corrosive observation that psychoanalysis is the disease of which it purports to be the cure. To Shelley, one must be both analyst and patient, sufferer and sympathetically ministering spirit.

Yet to describe mankind as Prometheus, rather than a poor ego in psychoanalysis, is, as I've suggested, to emphasize creative, redemptive power—self-making within art, rather than the more circumscribed Freudian hope for relative autonomy and stability. Shelley, contra Freud, suggests that Prometheus becomes more than a mere ego at the moment when he does not need the analyst any more, that the need for the analyst keeps you in the power cycle of master and slave, the cycle that Hegel, like Shelley, thought needed to be overcome for a spirit to enfranchise itself.

When Prometheus listens to himself what he hears is Jupiter talking. That is, Prometheus has been taken over, possessed, haunted. The situation is archetypally Gothic, for what is more redolent of deep haunting than to speak with another's voice, especially the master's? Perhaps, in fact, we do that much of the time; in a culture of rancor, if that is what we have, it will be characteristic of us, in our most charged moments, to sound like our antagonists when we plot our revenge against them. In a culture of rancor, which is just another way of saying a culture of Gothic, we are ever in danger of becoming ventriloquists' dummies. And if we repeat our S & M scripts in this way, how will there ever be anything new? A poet, a creator, a living man or woman who is not a revenant is, Shelley suggests, someone who can give up rancor, not someone who turns it into a principle of creation and of life.

For a nearly perfect antithesis to *Prometheus Unbound* one might turn to Edgar Allan Poe's remarkable story, "The Tell-Tale Heart." There the murderer ("True—nervous—very, very dreadfully nervous I had been and am; but why *will* you say that I am mad?") kills his innocent next-door neighbor, a man whom, the murderer protests, he has always liked.[11] Why does he kill the old man? It's the man's eye that haunts him. (It reminds the narrator of the eye of a vulture, which is, however coincidentally, the bird that Jupiter sends to torture Prometheus.) The accusatory gaze of the old man makes the murderer quake. But of course, Poe gives us to understand, the murderer is killing only an element of himself, that self-hating guilty element that he has temporarily succeeded in projecting outside, onto another.

Then, though his body is dismembered and buried beneath the floorboards, the heart of the victim begins, the narrator-killer swears, to rap away. The idea that the sound he hears, while the detectives are in the room questioning him, is his own guilty heartbeat, that idea is entirely unavailable to the killer. So too is the simple truth that in killing the old man he was attempting to kill some element of himself, the aching conscience, probably, that Freud was so intrigued by. But live for however long, the killer could never have that moment of self-recognition that Prometheus gets when he identifies Jupiter as an element in himself. Poe, dead-end Gothicist par excellence, couldn't believe in the possibility for such passionate self-discovery. Jung says somewhere that an observant person, passing us on the street, can tell us things about ourselves that it would take us a decade in psychoanalysis to learn. To which Poe would sneer: A decade, hah!

Prometheus wants to do to Jupiter something very much like what Jupiter is doing to him. The masochist has a sadist waiting inside. And he comes, in a flash, to understand that the way to be free of Jupiter—and of sadomasochism—is to release himself from the image of Jupiter within. And that requires forgiveness, a giving up of the spirit of revenge that's kept him on the mountain. "Words are quick and vain," says Prometheus. "Grief for awhile is blind, and so was mine. / I wish no living thing to suffer pain."[12]

Why is such forgiveness hard to generate? In part because Jupiter, the image of the negative god within, confers meaning on life. His existence as an antagonist stimulates energy, the energy of resistance, and gives it a focus. Jupiter also confers identity. Who is Prometheus? He is, at the start of the poem, the one who hates and is hated by Jupiter. And such hatred, which shrinks in its essence to a relation of lordship and bondage, gives shape to a life that cannot use religious faith or belief in historical destiny to achieve definitive meaning. Shelley deeply understands the pleasures of sadomasochism. He knows why we love it. And he does not think too well of himself to imagine that he's free of such drives. In a world without stable meanings, S & M provides some of the more solid ground we can find. This apparently avant-garde amoral form is in many ways a drive for long-lost assurances. Looking toward the present, we might remark that the local sadomasochist is probably the most up-to-date and the most nostalgic person on the block.

Jupiter is a specter, a ghost: he summarizes imperial desires, patriarchal cruelty, hatred for pleasure and sex, dumb misrule: but he also confers security. As long as Jupiter exists there will be someone around worth hating. But as Nietzsche, who greatly loved this poem (and whose interest in the subject of revenge as central to human life and identity may have been fired by his reading of it), taught, when you act in the spirit of revenge, you're acting in the present so as to change the meaning of the past. And for that reason your energies will forever be bound to prior events (which is one meaning of Prometheus's being in chains); your thoughts will be obsessions; you won't be able to do anything that is substantially fresh; you'll live posthumously.

Shelley, and Blake in poems like "The Crystal Cabinet," invite us to see that revenge is a self-defeating cycle: Prometheus becomes Jupiter becomes Prometheus until the end of time. Forgiveness is Shelley's way out of the spirit of revenge—that and the sexual love between equals that Prometheus and Asia embark on once Prometheus is free from his fixation, his compulsion to repeat. Embracing meaninglessness is Shelley's way of giving up S & M; or at least embracing the need to compound meanings of one's own. And the horror of no-meaning is part of what makes Gothic meaning, gruesome as it can be, so appealing.

To find a contemporary adolescent Shelleyanism—a redundancy, according to T. S. Eliot, who thought Shelley an eternal adolescent—we might glance back at the climactic moment of *Nightmare on Elm Street*. There our heroine Nancy, after realizing that none of the Elmstreetville adults are going to help her, goes off to the library and discovers a classic of horror-film pragmatism, a volume called *Booby Traps and Improvised Anti-Personnel Devices*. That and her boyfriend Glenn's riff about Balinese dream skills—if you see a monster in your dream turn your back on it (that sort of thing)—are her arsenal. Soon Nancy rigs up a whole Rube Goldberg assortment of tricks for Freddy, whom she lures out of his dream world and into suburbia. After blasting Krueger with a sledgehammer and setting him on fire, she's finally trapped by the beast up in her bedroom.

And there she does a sweetly adolescent rendering of Prometheus. Staring at Freddy, Nancy announces: "I take back every bit of energy I ever gave you; you're nothing." Then, turning her back and going sotto voce, "You're shit." And Freddy flames back into the void. Bad scriptwriting aside, the problem is that Nancy never really understands the part of herself that's most like Krueger, the part that's in love with suburbia and with repression, and that wants to adore her dad, the chief of police—the part that picked out her kittenish wardrobe, too, maybe. There's no full breakthrough into a new awareness. Just a shot in the dark; but it's the right time to shoot, and the right direction. Craven has some of Shelley's visionary instinct, just not Shelley's moral and intellectual force.

———————

How successful shall we judge Shelley to have been in his response to the Gothic? In one sense splendidly so. From Lewis and Radcliffe and their ilk, Shelley divines the centrality of haunting, the centrality of the Gothic predicament, and comprehends, as few others could, the deep allure of the S & M cycle in which many of us (I think) continue to live. Movingly, at least to me, he dramatizes a response to the spirit of revenge.

And yet maybe Shelley asks for too much at once. Perhaps the flaw in his great poem—he wrote it while he was still in his early twenties—lies in its wish to do away with revenge finally and for good, to get it all over with, now. For after *Prometheus Unbound* an odd thing happens. Shelley, having written his most hopeful great poem first, spends much of the rest of his career concocting other Jupiter-like monsters to be afflicted by. Crazy Count Cenci, the rapist of his daughter, and the chariot that leads the triumph of life (or the triumph of death in life) in his last poem are two Jupiter-like images that succeed Jupiter in Shelley's imagination. But to Cenci and the chariot, Shelley has no plausible renovating response. Having begun with a marvelous image of self-overcoming, Shelley wants to do it again and again. (So Freddy comes back at the end of *Nightmare*. Because Nancy doesn't really see her connection with him? Because Craven wants a sequel?) Overthrowing Jupiter, the right way, was probably the greatest imaginative achievement of Shelley's life.

On the lure of the drug rush, the best line I know of comes from the stand-up comic George Carlin: Cocaine, great stuff. It makes a new man out of you. Only one problem: new man wants a hit. Shelley, having thrown down Jupiter, seeks Jupiter again and again. The new man wants another hit—big hit. He wants to get to the top of the peak, then go there over and over, rather than conceiving of the S & M cycle as a temptation that's likely to persist, one that—the major discovery about it made—may have to be encountered in small, rather than grand and final ways.

Shelley's admirer, Nietzsche, also presumed to teach a way to break out of the Gothic prison. The tale in which Nietzsche initially relates this escape is itself Gothic, and at first sight looks like something much more akin to Poe than to Shelley. The tale seems to feature a visitation, in fact, by Poe's imp of the perverse, that inner sprite who nudges us toward self-ruining acts: "We perpetrate them," says Poe, "simply because we feel that we should *not*. Beyond or behind this, there is no intelligible principle."[13] After he's finished summarizing Nietzsche's Gothic tale, Martin Heidegger's first impulse is to speak of "a frightful prospect of a terrifying collective condition for beings in general." "Do we not," he asks, "confront the onset of dread?"[14]

Nietzsche's story is apparently simple. One night, in your "loneliest loneliness," a demon, a perverse imp, steals into the room and offers you the chance to repeat your life eternally. "This life as you now live it and have lived it," says the demon, "you will have to live once more and innumerable times more;

and there will be nothing new in it, but every pain and every joy and every thought and sigh and everything unutterably small or great in your life will have to return to you, all in the same succession and sequence—even this spider and this moonlight between the trees, and even this moment and I myself. The eternal hourglass of existence is turned upside down again and again, and you with it, speck of dust!"[15]

What the demon offers is, at least on first consideration, Gothic hell. It's a world where everything is past and there is nothing new, where no novelty whatsoever, not even the slightest glimmer, can possibly exist. It's the world of obsession, repetition, and grisly tedium that Poe's protagonists often inhabit. Here no one and nothing is ever young. Who would not greet the prospect of such a world with horror?

So Nietzsche's ultimate reaction to the demon's gambit seems almost mad. He grants that one's *initial* response to the offer would likely be horror. "Would you not throw yourself down and gnash your teeth and curse the demon who spoke thus?" But after a while, one might think better of it. For there could come, according to Nietzsche, a "tremendous moment" in which one would fall down and worship the imp as a god and thank him for his gift. "Never," Nietzsche imagines saying, "have I heard anything more divine." What Nietzsche suggests, it seems to me, is that one way out of the Gothic dilemma is through it. The way to overcome the spirit of repetition is by affirming repetition.

Nietzsche's further reflections on the spirit of revenge—inspired, I would speculate, by Shelley—reveal why this might be so. Revenge, says Nietzsche in *Zarathustra*, is "the will's ill will against time and its 'it was.'" Which means precisely what? Which means, I think, that the will, which can be the liberator and joy-bringer, according to Nietzsche, desires first to will backward. The will, out of resentment that so much has happened that it has not willed, that the self is a product of forces and accidents that it has had no shaping power over, strains to change the past.

It does so, one might speculate, in two ways. The first is through fantasy: through fantasy the will concocts images of a different past, one more glorious and rich, one where the self was indeed its own shaping force. The weakling becomes the hero, the loser transmogrifies into lover, and more. But the second mode of changing the past is more vigorous, both more promising and more ruinous, at least from Nietzsche's perspective. In the second mode, one tries to act in the present so as to change the past; one lives, in short, as Prometheus is determined to do when we see him first: for revenge. If Prometheus can humiliate Jupiter as Jupiter has Prometheus, and perhaps a little more, then Prometheus's humiliation never occurred. If the United States can do to Iraq what it ought to have done to North Vietnam, then the Vietnam War never happened.

So far, Nietzsche and Shelley concur about the dynamics of revenge—and about the centrality of this, the ultimate Gothic malady. But Nietzsche's response is stranger and subtler than Shelley's. Nietzsche's response is to lie. We overcome revenge, and put ourselves in the position to be delighted by the imp's offer—though not to accept it—Nietzsche never says we ought to do *that*—when we can look back at the past and say, "Thus I willed it." That is, we stop being victims, Gothic victims, when we say that everything that has happened to us was for the best, and that we wouldn't have had it any other way.

Once you've told that lie, and it is a lie, you put yourself in a position to reveal new truths, in that what you do in the present and future is unchained from the past. You're not trying to undo prior traumas any more. The new book isn't composed to redeem former errors, to correct bad impressions, to compensate for sins. It's written in freedom, with no obsessive prior commitments attached to it.

The anti-Gothic Gothic charm of willing the eternal recurrence can also provide a pragmatic standard for the life to come. That is: only do it—whatever *it* is—if you'd be willing to do it over and over again eternally. Suppose this were the standard for our acts, this necessity of then repeating them forever. But in a sense, if we have only one life, then all acts we commit here have the same eternal status—this life is all there is and all there will be for us, so why not try to live it as such?

Nietzsche, unlike the grander Shelley, wants to grapple with the minute particulars of existence. To be exalted by the imp is to be committed to small-scale repudiation of revenge, not just the big operatic gesture that's initially sublime and ultimately frustrating: new man wants a hit.

So Nietzsche takes the darkest Gothic vision—the one that's manifest in Poe by virtue of the fact that most of his stories are finished from the first page—and pushes through it into a visionary affirmation of a life that passes beyond the sadomasochistic cycle. Most of us can only glimpse that kind of post-Gothic affirmation. Most of us would tell the demon to go to hell. But in his fable, and in the reflections on revenge and the eternal recurrence that traverse his work, Nietzsche has let us glimpse what a life without revenge, a life that had defeated the Gothic in its own most profound terms, might *feel* like. Who knows how many other visions there could be of this kind of overcoming? If Shelley and Nietzsche seem in some ways inadequate—surely, at the very least, their Gothic predicaments are not quite ours—perhaps they're on the right track. They refuse to leave the Gothic drive uncontested.

In our moment, we find virtually no cogent opposition to the Gothic mind at all. There's Forrest Gump, Bly's Iron John, and Bradshaw's inner child on the one side—ephemeral reactions to a culture of despair. These works cannot find, much less confront, a cogent Gothic opposition. On the other side, there is a strong, and comprehensively ramified Gothic vision that runs from Anne Rice's latest phantasmagoria to the evening news. Poe is lord (if there is a lord) in contemporary culture, and he has no challenger of Shelley's or Nietzsche's ilk, no one who can effectively bring the Gothic and visionary drives together in memorable images of mental fight. As a culture, we seem to have lost touch with the play of Gothic and visionary that characterized some of the major nineteenth-century writers at their best.

One way to describe Shelley's Jupiter is to say that he is a Gothic villain ramified with large-scale meanings. As a boy, Shelley wrote a pair of Gothic novels, *Zastrozzi* and *St. Irvyne*, and the idiom of Gothic was never far from his mind. All that Ambrosio and Montoni suggest as Gothic hero-villains—the triumph of aristocracy, of superstition, of power over reason—all of those tendencies are made manifest, but more emphatically and passionately, in Jupiter. Radcliffe and Lewis allow us to see their hero-villains as much different from ourselves, as foreign and strange. But Shelley, anticipating Freud, wants us to see the Gothic oppressor as an interior force, a part of the self that we treasure. Shelley is willing to indict the audience that Lewis and Radcliffe addressed much more cordially.

The major English visionary poets, all of whom read Mrs. Radcliffe and Monk Lewis, found more than entertainment in productions like *Mysteries of Udolpho*, *The Italian*, and *The Monk*. They found a vocabulary in Gothic that was apt to their purpose, which was, to put it simply, to create plausible visions of human renewal. In the Gothic idiom, writers like Shelley, Blake, Keats, and, in a rather complex way, Wordsworth found a litany of images for all that they wanted to struggle against in their drive to redescribe, and in redescribing perhaps to remake, human consciousness. They found figures of resistance to their self-remaking aspirations. They found images for what possessed them, needless limits to which they—and perhaps their readers—were chained. In the Gothic mode, they found what weakly visionary productions like *Forrest Gump* and *Iron John* lack: images of all in the psyche that hates change, that loves *significant* pain, or better, pleasure-pain, that attracts us to the compulsion to repeat because, distasteful as it may be, it rams life full with meaning.

Scholars of the period almost unanimously affirm that a consequential cultural shift in the West occurred with the Revolution in France. Finding a consensus on the precise nature of that shift, though, is another matter. Leslie Fiedler describes the transformation not in terms of a Romantic literary movement per se, but of something much larger. Fiedler speaks simply, and dramatically, of "the Break-through":

> The Break-through is characterized not only by the separation of psychology from philosophy, the displacement of the traditional leading genres by the personal lyric and analytic prose fiction (with the consequent subordination of plot to character); it is also marked by the promulgation of a theory of revolution as a good in itself and, most notably perhaps, by a new concept of inwardness. One is almost tempted to say, by the invention of a new kind of self, a new level of mind; for what has been happening since the eighteenth century seems more like the development of a new organ than the mere finding of a new way to describe old experience.[16]

Fielder rightly emphasizes the growing sense that human beings contain not one self or two but, at least potentially, many. The Freudian theory of the id and Jung's of a collective unconscious are late flowerings of the visionary's perception, richer in many ways because as yet uncodified, that the inner life is shifting, complex, variable, many voiced.

And Fiedler is right, too, in his emphasis on revolution. For beginning in the late eighteenth century total upheaval, on the social level, but also on the personal, becomes more and more a periodically desirable event. Crises, private and public, become the perceived means for truly salutary change. Images of fracture, sudden metamorphosis, and violent birth begin to replace Augustan visions of organic cohesion. Of this revolutionary legacy Karl Marx (who began his writing life as a poet, composing among other things Shelleyan versions of Prometheus) is the major inheritor.

The focus on inwardness (Harold Bloom says that Americans only feel that they are truly themselves when they are alone) and the conviction that crisis has become (paradoxically enough) a permanent and defining condition of life are pervasive in our fin-de-siècle culture, and they are products of the Break-through. (These are, of course, only two major legacies from the late eighteenth and early nineteenth centuries; a full catalogue of our cultural continuities with that period would have no end.) The amount of commentary that the Breakthrough has received, and that it continues to merit, is daunting. What makes the task both pressing and of a peculiar difficulty is the strong possibility that we still live within the values and assumptions that the transition from the neoclassical period spawned. What remains to be done is to see (if we can) how our own 1990s cultural vocabularies relate to those that in many ways originated them, to see what we can learn from our progenitors.

The visionary writers—it was the Victorians who gave them the misleading and now mildly derogatory name Romantics—tended to accept the key premise of Gothic, that to be human is to be haunted. The haunting agent that Shelley called Jupiter, and that Nietzsche later was to associate with the spirit of revenge, had different names for all of the Romantic writers. Blake speaks of the Specter, the throttling creature that suffocates the imagination by enforcing fear, accommodation, conformity, the desire for success and acceptance in the most standard terms. For Keats—who once spoke of "mother Radcliffe"—the figure of inner haunting is called the Identity or Selfhood, the figure of fear that keeps the imagination from flying free into the kind of identification with others that Keats celebrated in Shakespeare and famously described in terms of Negative Capability.

Coleridge, who avidly read and reviewed both Radcliffe and Lewis, is the most haunted of the visionary poets. But unlike Blake and Shelley (and Nietzsche), he never arrives at a cogent way to overcome the spirit of limitation and fear that's embodied by his specters. The Man from Porlock, the Gothic messenger who comes to halt the composition of "Kubla Khan," turns up in a variety of guises throughout Coleridge's work, choking off his imagination's finest flight. Much of Coleridge's major poetry dramatizes the defeat of the visionary urge at the expense of Gothic energies—which makes Coleridge the most frustrating of poets, and also one of the most valuable, since he goes further than almost anyone else before Freud in showing us the precise shape of our Gothic fears. He martyred his talents to a profound vision of what inhibits creative change.

Wordsworth is by far the most complex of all the visionaries in his response to the Gothic. Overtly he hated the form. In "The Preface to the Lyrical Ballads," he dismissed Gothic as base entertainment; it was the sort of thing that people pent in cities, their nerves deadened by the need to seal themselves against excess stimulation, might require to be roused, however briefly, into some semblance of felt life. (How much like our own motives for attending to Oprah and O. J.) Wordsworth despised Monk Lewis.

But Wordsworth also sets his first greatly inward poem in Lewis's terrain, not far from a ruined monastery. "Tintern Abbey" is a poem about what one might do when the abbeys have been destroyed by time, by rebellious upheaval, or by the powers of skepticism. Wordsworth, like the Gothic writers Leslie Fiedler describes, is haunted by the destruction of the paternal past, ecclesiastical and aristocratic. He is ambivalent about the mind's enlightened victory over purported superstition. But instead of summoning up the patriarchal ghosts that abide in his mind, as Shelley does, and trying to purge them fully, to make the mind entirely unhaunted, Wordsworth accepts haunting as the ultimate fate of post-revolutionary humanity, or at least as *his* fate. The past, as signified by the form of that ruined abbey, will inevitably bear down on the present. The Gothic bind is ineluctable.

What one can do is to accept the fact of inevitable haunting, but shift the terms. Wordsworth's poetry is the poetry of self-haunting. He's haunted by the former self, the childhood self, rather than by the collective past. If the mind must be possessed, let it be possessed by its own past experiences, not by nostalgia and guilt over monks, counts, and all they represent. Let us be the victims and also the shaping artists of our Gothic experience. From this perspective, Shelley asks for too much. He wants complete freedom from haunting. Wordsworth accepts the inevitable, but changes its shape—and in doing so shifts our sense of what it is to be human.

And what about the much-castigated Emerson? Can we see him, too, in the context of the Gothic/visionary writers who came before him in England? Or is he, as the Gothic mind avers, the true progenitor to Forrest Gump, Iron John, and the Women Who Run with Wolves, along with such preachers of self-reliance as Henry Ford and Ronald Reagan?

Emerson is an exquisitely subtle writer and a very tough one—as sweet as barbed wire, A. Bartlett Giamatti once called him. To be sure, Emerson is a philosopher of novelty, of the American capacity to begin anew; but the cost for such innovation, he continually informs us, can be appalling, and it is a cost that each must bear himself. For Emerson demonstrates again and again how we are confined by those things in our lives that we love most truly. Not social evil, not outward oppression, but our own most cherished commitments are what most often stagnate our spirits. They prevent us from breaking into fresh perception, expression, and overall achievement. Our friends, children, lovers, and families, the books we've read, the natural vistas that give us ease, foreign travel, human joys of all sorts tend to tranquilize us, lead us into serene death in life.

Emerson's writing perpetually dramatizes withdrawal from such delimiting, loving commitments. When his dear boy Waldo dies, he brutally and expeditiously takes back his emotional investment from the child, comparing the loss of the boy to the loss of an expensive piece of real estate. Emerson demeans his loss, and in so doing gets it further behind him.

Freud described mourning as a process of bringing up each memory and expectation that attached the mourner to the beloved, then hypercathecting and dismissing them one by one. The process, says Freud, is generally carried out over a long period of time and at great expense of libidinal energy. Emerson does not have the time to mourn in the scrupulous Freudian fashion; he wants his energies restored as quickly as possible. Emerson, in short, refuses mourning, or strains to make short work of it. And what is mourning if not a form of haunting, the Gothic condition? For mourning, seen from Emerson's perspective, is nothing more than being possessed by a past that no longer truly exists, worshipping a ghost.

It greatly pains Emerson to withdraw his energies from moribund investments, investments that don't pay returns in vital force. Yet he continually counsels himself (and us) to pull

out of dead churches, dead schools, all objects (persons included) that don't repay our allegiances at a profit, and to return
the energies of the self to the self for redeployment. Though
such self-exorcism may hurt, Emerson bears the pain because he
wants the freedom to experience the world freshly that having a
surplus of emotional and erotic energy at one's disposal confers.
Emerson is perpetually recognizing how much he is haunted by
the past—how fully he's possessed—and then exorcising himself. So it's not surprising that when we look at what the Gothic
intelligence tells us is a facile piece of Emersonian optimism,
"Self-Reliance," we encounter a world of Gothic imagery:
chains and prisons, slavery, shadows, giants, corpses and the
like, all of which figure Emerson's bondage to the past. But it's a
self-inflicted bondage, Emerson asserts, and it's only by one's
own exertions—by identifying and dismissing deadening investments—that one can be, if only temporarily, free.

Poe and his descendants don't see this side of Emerson at all;
to a Gothic master like Robert Penn Warren, Emerson is only
plausible when read on an airplane, flying high above the dark,
bloody American ground. To Poe, Emerson is just a Yankee
transcendentalist, with no sense of evil, no sense of sin. But
Emerson does have a sense of sin; it's simply a more ruthless
sense than Poe, who prided himself on his worldliness, could
ever have conceived. To Emerson "the only sin is limitation"—the only sin is Gothic bondage to the past. You sin, in
other words, when you take Poe's universe of death as the end
of the story. Emerson referred to Poe once as "the jingle man,"
thinking probably of "The Raven" and "Annabel Lee." But
Emerson had the right to his derision; jingles aside, Emerson
contains a great deal of Poe. He understands the despair and
grief that Poe—who mourned for everything, sometimes even
before it died—rendered; he just won't rest content within it.
But if Emerson contains Poe, Poe, for his part, is far from
encompassing Emerson.

Woodstock, and much that went with it, could surely have used a dose of Emerson's harsh wisdom. For recall how 1960s-style visionary impulses could so easily be undermined by Gothic eruptions. In *The Texas Chainsaw Massacre*, we see that the '60s generation had not overcome the reign of Saturn (the figure who plays the role of Shelley's Jupiter for Tobe Hooper) and his cannibal progeny, but had merely moved the show out of their ken, temporarily. The benevolent farmers who appear all through *Woodstock* to proclaim that—as The Who liked to say—the kids are all right, reappear in *TCM* as the horrible clan of country folk primed to devour the children of peace and love. These are the poor, mutant, and mean who weren't invited to the party at Max's farm and who would have gone into a frenzy if they were. They're the ones that the flower children couldn't find a place for. And of course they also embody the drives for destruction that were perhaps alive, if unrecognized, in the kids themselves, and that came on later at Altamont, in the Weather Underground, and in the Symbionese Liberation Army.

Sixties visionary art mattered much more than what one finds in *Forrest Gump*, for its ends were larger and nobler. Sixties visionaries wanted pleasure and harmony, ease, more enjoyment, less anxiety, the kinds of liberation that Friedrich Schiller and, following him, Herbert Marcuse associated with the aesthetic realm. *Gump* is about personal gain. Blake, who would have had only contempt for Forrest and his ilk, would have delighted in Woodstock as a Beulah land of easy pleasures: not an end in itself, but a means to a worthwhile end—a vacation away from the necessary specter, Urizen or Nobodaddy or Leatherface, who would have to be invoked and dealt with in time.

I am writing in compressed terms here. Another volume, scholarly and comprehensive, would be needed to fully connect the visionaries of two hundred years ago, and those of the 1960s, to the Gothic tradition. But that might be a consequential book, in that it could persuade us that the visionary writers often knew what our culture has forgotten: that the purposes of cultural vitality ask for a conjunction of dark and renovating energies, that the two traditions, now split, might be joined once more. What Blake and Emerson, Herbert Marcuse and Norman O. Brown, and above all, I think, Percy Bysshe Shelley understood is that one must face the Gothic antagonist, Poe's principle of death, if one wishes to achieve imaginative life.

As it is, twentieth-century American criticism of visionary poetry has been symptomatic of our age. It has focused, often subtly, on the self-renewing drive but ignored, or displaced, the visionary poets' fixation with Gothic horror. When in the 1960s and '70s a group of brilliant scholars, among them M. H. Abrams, Geoffrey Hartman, and Harold Bloom, set out to rehabilitate the visionary writers from T. S. Eliot's charge that they were a herd of adolescents and Matthew Arnold's that they didn't know enough (unlike himself), it's not surprising that the scholars found exalted grounds for understanding their beloved poets, making them look much more respectable than they were. To this generation of critics, the visionaries resembled Biblical prophets who had somehow been reborn in eighteenth-century England.

Abrams saw them as naturalizing the Christian tradition, preserving contact with a numinous realm of experience, but bringing it into this world through what he called "natural supernaturalism." Hartman was absorbed by the ways that Wordsworth's consciousness moved from sublimity, a sense of fearful deific power, to tranquility within temperate nature. From early on Bloom was obsessed with the Romantics' drive to rewrite Milton. Eventually this interest grew into a psycho-analytic theory of poetic influence, in which precursor poets haunt living artists, blocking their drive for originality.

Bloom's best-known book, *The Anxiety of Influence,* is not entirely unlike a Gothic novel, arguing as it does that the Romantics were possessed by past poets—spectral blocking agents—whose originality they feared. The precursor haunts the new poet, or ephebe. He inhabits the ephebe's unconscious, compelling him to repeat his most potent tropes even when the ephebe believes himself to be at the height of his creative powers. Or the precursor blocks the ephebe completely, becoming what Bloom, borrowing a term from Blake, calls the Covering Cherub. "The Covering Cherub," Bloom writes, "is a demon of continuity: his baleful charm imprisons the present in the past, and reduces a world of differences into a grayness of uniformity."[17] The Cherub, like a demon out of Poe, renders life damned, doomed, and dismal from the start by enforcing repetition, enforcing the past.

Bloom is brilliantly right about haunting, about the Gothic element in visionary poetry, but he displaces it in a peculiar fashion. As we've seen, the visionaries are chiefly haunted by specters of their own creation, and those specters have all of the political, aesthetic, and ethical ramifications, and then much more, that the Gothic authors invested in their hero-villains. Coleridge is haunted and never finds deliverance: in "Kubla Khan" he is obsessed by the man from Porlock; in "The Eolian Harp" by his wife Sara, who suppresses his sexy, strange reveries, asserting her orthodox Christianity against his polymorphously perverse nature-worship. But Blake and Shelley are haunted by specters whom they eventually overthrow, more or less believably. In effect, Bloom displaces the Gothic element in the visionary poets' best work, claiming that it's a hidden dynamic (hidden indeed from the poets themselves), rather than the overt and central theme that it is.

These critics were right to see the visionaries as being deeply engaged in a play between opposing forces—their poetry at its best is dialectical. And right too that the poets negotiated and renegotiated their self-identities through what Blake called mental fight. But it's also no surprise that they ignore the Gothic writers, by whom the so-called high Romantics were transfixed. It surely can't be a pleasure for the serious scholar to be reminded that some of the greatest poets in English are kin to the creators of *The Mysteries of Udolpho* and *The Monk*, and to the makers of *Psycho* and *The Texas Chainsaw Massacre*, too. But they are. They are the kin who want to transform the terrible visions of their Gothic contemporaries, but on those visions they crucially rely.

In 1872, Friedrich Nietzsche published what may be his most influential book, *The Birth of Tragedy*. There he argues that the apogee of culture had come with the pre-Euripidean tragic writers, who had triumphantly interfused Apollonian and Dionysian energies. The Apollonian in Nietzsche is form-giving, detached, beautiful; the Dionysian wild, destructive and creative at once. To combine the two visions is to achieve a passionate wisdom: the Dionysian gives access to the ferocious amorality of the life and death drives, both within ourselves and abroad; the Apollonian dispenses just enough formal distance, enough grace, for us to bear the Dionysian flux with something like serenity.

But the interanimation of the two forces is eventually undone by the onset of the cerebral, analytic culture brought on by Socrates. To Nietzsche, Socrates' cold eye burned through every myth, reducing all phenomena to abstract, analytical terms. "His mission," says Nietzsche, was "to make existence appear intelligible and thereby justified."[18] But the Dionysian, Nietzsche insists, cannot be rendered intelligible, at least not without falsification. Dionysus is too encompassing and chaotic to be understood, though our wish to turn away from his force and stem our confusion makes us ready to affirm the reductions offered by Socrates and his extensive progeny. We readily embrace what Nietzsche calls "the grand metaphysical illusion," which affirms "that thought, guided by the thread of causation, might plumb the farthest abysses of being and even *correct* it."[19] What's lost in such reduction is contact with those irrational forces that, if dangerous, are also vital. We become cadavers or walking ghosts, Nietzsche claims, when we deny Dionysian force.

For the Anglo-American visionary authors, we might say, Apollo and Dionysus are replaced by the transformative drive and the Gothic. (If we want to stay within the realm of myth, we might speak of Prometheus and Jupiter.) As the Socratic is a debased form of the Apollonian (Socratism, as Nietzsche has it, is rigorous and rule-bound, but without the musical grace of the authentically Apollonian), so our current Gothic might be understood as a debased residue of the richer Gothic forms to be found in Lewis, Shelley, and Blake. Our own Gothic—no-fault, dead-end, without social throw-weight—hasn't the power to push its audience into fresh perceptions. And too we seem to have lost contact with the promise of Gothic and visionary interanimation that Freud gestures toward at the end of *Civilization and Its Discontents*.

In England, George Gordon, Lord Byron, who greatly influenced Poe, probably did more than anyone to undermine the dialectic of the Gothic and renovating drives. As the great critic Arnold Hauser puts it, "Byron externalizes and trivializes the spiritual problems of romanticism; he makes a social fashion of the spiritual disintegration of his time . . . Byron bestows a seductive charm on the curse of his generation and turns his heroes into exhibitionists who openly display their wounds, into masochists who publicly load themselves with guilt and shame, flagellants who torment themselves with self-accusations and pangs of conscience and confess both their evil and their good deeds with the same intellectual pride of ownership."[20] In short, Byron turns the crises that propelled the visionaries to encounter the Gothic into a sequence of stylized gestures.

Byron, it's said, learned to sneer from Ann Radcliffe's Schedoni, hero-villain of *The Italian,* and indeed the dashing Byronic persona is, as Northrop Frye affirms, greatly indebted to the mental workings of the shy, asthmatic woman who invented a major form of English Gothic.[21] But Byron did not do with the Gothic hero-villains what Blake and Shelley did—infuse them with existential force, ramify them profoundly. Rather, Byron made the Gothic hero-villain into a bourgeois attraction, the merely interesting man. For if Byron is himself the hero-villain of his work—an original enough stroke—he never confronts what's darkest in himself with a transforming urge.

Byron lacked all capacity for introspection. He had a sharp, mercurial mind, capable of lightning response to events, but he had the analytic ability of a songbird. As Northrop Frye puts it, "His extroversion made him easily confused by efforts at self-analysis, and he flew into rages when he was accused of any lack of feeling. One reason why his marriage demoralized him so was that it forced such efforts on him."[22]

And what is darkest in the Byronic hero is not really very dark. He cannot see deeply enough, look with sufficient coldness, to reveal anything truly disturbing. Byron is forever playing at evil. He's sentimental, shallow, always posturing, never conveying the intensity of precursors like Hamlet, or even of Ambrosio. The Byronic hero is charismatic, but thoroughly conventional and small-scale in all of his crises and woes. He performs the role of alluring aristocrat to the philistine middle classes. Without intellectual capability, without emotional nuance, the wildly popular Byronic figure cheapens the image of the Gothic hero-villain, and makes the serious Gothic-visionary encounter that much less tenable. Byron, in a sense, stands in relation to the more arresting Gothic hero-villains as Bradshaw's inner child does to Shelley's Prometheus.

In *Don Juan,* Byron finally finds a style that fits his temperament, the style of skimming, of quick forward movement, the verse flying on as a stone skims across water. He never stops to ponder or to engage experience in consequential ways. The poetry moves with a wonderful celerity, witty, sure of itself, superficial. Camille Paglia observes that "in their exuberance, hedonism, and mannered irrelevance, the Beach Boys epitomize the self-sustaining and annoyingly self-congratulatory youth culture that Byron began."[23]

Byron had what Freud would call a stunningly mobile libido. He was able to shift commitments of psychic energy with the speed that an accomplished trader can move futures on the floor of the Exchange. Byron never rests where he might be caught out and made to commit himself. He's always on the move, always changing—in part out of a fear of being confronted for the opportunist that he is. He's radically attractive, but loves no one but himself. Shelley, Byron's friend, exhibited what Robert Frost describes as the will's capacity to throw itself into a project, into a vision, and then, at the end, to determine whether its energies have been strongly spent or lost. "Strongly spent," says Frost, "is synonymous with kept." Shelley would say that strongly spent is better than kept by far. Byron never spends anything: before you know that he's extended his force, he's taken it all back and gone on his way.

Byron turns the idiom of the Gothic into the stuff of Hollywood entertainment; his persona influences every cheaply alienated actor from Humphrey Bogart to Jack Nicholson, as well as the femme fatale. In his vision of life as endless irony (for what is irony but the expressed unwillingness to render a full investment in one's beliefs or relations?), he offers a deconstruction of the various modes of mental strife that Blake and Shelley and Emerson practice. He's a progenitor of everything in the Anglo-American mind that's attracted to our various postmodernisms, predicting and endorsing the world of parody, cut-up, pastiche, mime, impersonation, repetition, surface flash, and ceaseless movement. (If David Letterman could rhyme, he'd be a second-tier Byron.) Byron saps the potential for Gothic and visionary conjunction, leading culture toward a new age in which wisdom lies in the art of sliding well on surfaces. In the current cultural imagination, one of Gothic's main alternatives is the skimming mode manifest in the postmodern culture of unabated irony.

———

Yet if one looks long enough it is possible to see some fin-de-siècle stirrings of the visionary/Gothic dialectic that this book has described. Tony Kushner and Toni Morrison are both consequential Gothic writers who strain impressively to be more than that. In their work we can see some of the harsh inhibitions that now beset us, as well, perhaps, as some cues for future renovation.

In *Angels in America: A Gay Fantasia on National Themes*, playwright Tony Kushner concocts a marvelous Gothic hero-villain. Roy Cohn, detest him as one must, makes the play. Things light up when he comes on stage. As the literary critic Ross Posnock puts it, Cohn "commandeers the play, inspiring its most powerful writing and dwarfing the absorbing but largely familiar domestic subplots unfolding around him."[24] When we first meet power-crazed Cohn, he's doing a virtuoso improvisation on a bank of phones, leaping from one conversation to another, intimidating, wheedling, pleading, deal-making, postponing, and hustling, for the edification of one Joe Pitt, his Mormon protégé, who looks on in awe. Cohn is burning with his greed and hunger: "I wish I was an octopus, a fucking octopus. Eight loving arms and all those suckers. Know what I mean?"[25]

Cohn, lawyer and New York power-broker, is Kushner's Jupiter, though with a raw charisma that dull Jupiter, prototype of every boring dictator (the word suggests a nonstop talker working in constant monotone), isn't close to matching. Cohn is a man of stature: he is not, he asserts, a *homosexual*. He's not defined by the conventional labels. It's not "who I fuck or who fucks me," he insists, "but who will pick up the phone when I call, who owes me favors. This is what a label refers to. Now to someone who does not understand this, homosexual is what I am because I have sex with men. But really this is wrong . . . Homosexuals are men who in fifteen years of trying cannot get a pissant antidiscrimination bill through City Council. Homosexuals are men who know nobody and who nobody knows. Who have zero clout."[26]

Cohn is long on clout—he's corrupt, a deal-maker; also long on energy and life force. (On the AIDS quilt he gets the epithets "Coward. Bully. Victim.") He's the character that all of the up-to-date gay men in the play want to be as unlike as possible, the monster incarnate. Roy Cohn, says the guilt-weighed liberal, Louis Ironson, "he's like the polestar of human evil, he's like the worst human being who ever lived, he isn't *human* even, he's . . . "[27]

Redemption, in *Millennium Approaches*, the first of the play's two parts, is what's at issue—redemption from AIDS and from the empire of Roy Cohn, his pal Ronald Reagan, and all they embody. Such redemption, if it's coming at all, seems likely to be coming from the angels, the heavenly polymorphous perverts who make visitations to Prior Walter, trying to persuade him that they have prophetic news to deliver and that he's to be their medium. And so audiences returned for Part Two, *Perestroika*, in which they reasonably expected to learn what the angels had in mind. But Tony Kushner isn't William

Blake or John Milton. He doesn't know how to prophesy, at least through the mouth of a visitant angel. Apparently none came to his garden to consort with him, as the angel did with Blake.

In *Perestroika*, Kushner's angels turn out to be a bunch of duds. They hate change, movement, hybridity, action, miscegenation: they want everyone to stay put. Since their God skipped town, they've been helpless to recommend anything to humanity except an abject caution: they counsel us to become Nietzsche's Last Men and Women and to begin hopping, blinking, and savoring small pleasures forthwith.

If there's a prophet to be found in *Perestroika*, it's not going to be an angel, and it's not Prior Walter, though he does eventually get to enjoy some peculiar sex with one among the heavenly hosts. Rather it's Belize, a black former drag queen. Or to be more precise, it's Belize in a strange sort of collaboration with Roy Cohn.

Belize is an ideal, maybe an idealized, figure, sensible, hip, funny, well-traveled through the Dantesque social strata of New York. He's also a nurse. In that capacity, Belize encounters Cohn, and a relationship that begins in antipathy moves toward a certain mutual regard. For what Cohn possesses is, it turns out, what the AIDS-racked gay men and their friends most need: the will for more life. They are all more humane than Cohn, more cultivated, more generous; but he's tougher than they are. He wants to live forever. In fact, Cohn dies three or four times in the play, or seems to. Each time it looks like he's finally succumbed to AIDS-induced maladies, he kicks himself back up for one more round. He's like the villain in a slasher movie, Jason, or Freddy, or Michael Myers; nothing can quite put him away.

At the end of the play, when many of the characters we're supposed to have come to care for are sitting around Bethesda Fountain in Central Park, we see that the wish for more life is the one thing that—contra the inertia-preaching angels—all can get together to affirm. And it is, it seems, Cohn's rhapsody about his own hunger to stay in the world that impresses Belize enough to offer him some medical advice that saves him, at least for a while. In a memorable speech to Belize, Cohn compares his own avidity for life to that of a bunch of persistent crab lice he once contracted. In the same oration, Cohn, who in life vehemently denied he was gay, going on periodically about fags and their turpitude, comes out of the closet. It's the mixture of crazy life force and vulnerability that arrests Belize and opens him up to Cohn.

Or so one might reasonably gather from the exchange: Belize himself seems baffled as to why he's helping Cohn out, telling him to get into a fledgling AZT program and, once in, to make sure he's not part of the fifty percent stuck with placebos. "Why are you telling me this?" "I wish I knew," Belize says.[28] And in a sense, the play doesn't know either.

As Posnock suggests, Kushner seems determined to humanize Roy Cohn, to bring him, somehow, into the circle of good gay friends. Kushner wants Cohn to be forgiven by the group of buddies; indeed a few of them gather around the monster—once he's *finally* dead—to say Kaddish. But Cohn wouldn't want to be forgiven, not by anyone, but least of all not by a bunch of progressive gay men; Cohn was an aspiring over-man and immoralist, a figure that Christopher Marlowe, creator of Tamburlaine and Barabas, should have been alive to render. He was anything but a good secular humanist.

Belize—referred to, in Blakean enough language, as Cohn's "negation" and his "shadow"—eventually rises to a form of prophecy in Cohn's presence.[29] His Utopia is a "big city, overgrown with weeds, but flowering weeds. On every corner a wrecking crew and something new and crooked going up catty-corner to that . . . Piles of trash, but lapidary like rubies and obsidian, and diamond-colored cowspit streamers in the wind. And voting booths . . . And everyone in Balenciaga gowns with red corsages, and big dance palaces full of music and lights and racial impurity and gender confusion . . . And all the deities are creole, mulatto, brown as the mouths of rivers. Race, taste and history finally overcome. And you ain't there."[30]

Belize's heaven isn't bad for a start, but in a play that claims a prophetic license, it's disappointing that this is the best that Kushner can do. Belize-heaven is appealing, but also stylized and under-evoked, thin. It's concocted to please himself and a few friends, and virtually no one else. And Roy Cohn's not there. Which is another way of saying that despite the well-rendered moment of connection between Cohn and Belize (which perhaps kicked Belize into the prophetic mode to begin with), Cohn's forgotten when it comes time to formulate the play's regenerative vision. His cruelty has no place in the future society, but neither does his charisma, his energy, his drive. All they do in Belize-heaven is party; in Cohn heaven, you make things (and mar them).

Kushner is too much in the propaganda mode, too much into making us love his gay characters, to let them see into the dark heart of Cohn and find themselves there (as Shelley finds himself in Jupiter) in any significant way. At the close of the play, all of the sentimentality flows over when Prior Walter turns to the audience and says:

> Bye now.
> You are all fabulous creatures, each and every one.
> And I bless you: *More Life*.
> The Great Work Begins.[31]

Worthy of Tiny Tim, this ending: Bless us, each and every one. Having stood up to repudiate the American angel craze, observing to *Time* that that's not what his work is about at all,

Kushner here sounds like one of its more redoubtable shills. Finally, the bad old past as embodied by Cohn is gone. The witch is dead (wicked old witch). There's no worry that we—young, free, and out—will ever come to resemble the grand ogre.

Or possess what's most compelling in Roy Cohn, either, his astounding vitality. Without some purchase on what Cohn embodies, the rattling on about more life comes to nought. *Angels in America* draws a marvelous Gothic character, but it never takes its own Gothic wisdom seriously; it fails to dramatize how one might appropriate what's most potent and productive in Cohn, while sloughing the rest away. The play can't manage to be—though it pretends it is—both an advertisement for the common humanity of gay men, sentimental enough to thrive on Broadway, and a hard look into its characters' uglier precincts, a drama of persuasive change.

———

About the dark side of America, its horrific past, Toni Morrison, another remarkable Gothic artist, is relentlessly candid. Her post–Civil War novel *Beloved* begins with a troubling riddle: the people in America who feel most ashamed about slavery were, and are, African Americans. Morrison's black characters are virtually all filled with guilt and self-loathing not because of what they did, but because of the horrible things done to them. What must I be to have been treated so? They are all haunted by slavery, as Sethe's house is haunted by the ghost of Beloved, the child she murdered so that she wouldn't be taken back into slavery. Sethe does it with a blade. *Beloved* is a slasher novel, though it is a good deal more than that.

The critic Stanley Crouch wrote against *Beloved* with something close to fury. He sees Morrison as a major player in the victim sweepstakes. One quickly understands that what Crouch dislikes in Morrison may be as much her willingness to express and evoke emotion—Crouch's aesthetic reminds one of Hemingway's—as her dramatic argument. But unlike most readers, white readers in particular, who can bring themselves to swoon about Morrison's evocation of the human condition (or something like that), Crouch knows that what's at stake in *Beloved* is the historical relations between blacks and whites in America. The novel seeks to produce a dislocation of national consciousness on the subject of race.

Crouch sees this immediately in the dedication, "Sixty Million and more," which is, Crouch points out, six million times ten (and more). That is, Morrison wants us to know that slavery resulted in the death of about ten times more Africans than the Holocaust did Jews. Then Crouch goes on to draw out the similarities between *Beloved* and a Holocaust documentary: "As a holocaust novel, it includes disenfranchisement, brutal transport, sadistic guards, failed and successful escapes, murder, liberals among the oppressors, a big war, underground cells, separation of family members, losses of loved ones to the violence of the mad order and characters who, like the Jew in *The Pawnbroker*, have been made emotionally catatonic by the past."[32] Crouch sees Morrison as out to compare losses with the Jews, as entering into a competition with them for sympathy and high victim-status, but that's not quite right.

Rather I understand Morrison as saying something like this. You white Americans have an event in your past that is entirely comparable to the Holocaust. Your ancestors did it (in all probability), and if they didn't, you even now are living off the fruits of it. How do you feel about Germany? Do you feel that they still have some owning up to do? That they may have reparations to make? That they delude themselves? Well, all of these questions now have to be applied to yourself, white reader.

In fact a critical segment of white culture, up to Herrenstein and Murray with their findings on IQ and race, might be seen as concocting ways to denigrate the people who were brutalized, to make them look bad. Morrison's Schoolteacher, the monster who measures the heads of the slaves and has his sons note down Sethe's human and her animal characteristics in separate columns, is part of a venerable tradition. He's providing extenuating evidence, so that whites can feel released. They weren't quite human. It didn't really count.

Stamp Paid is the moral imagination of Morrison's book, much as Belize is of Kushner's play. He's a comprehensively decent man, who risks his life for others, and who is revered, just about universally, in the black community. (He's "not felt a trickle of meanness his whole adult life"; "All his visits were beneficial" so "his step or holler through a doorway got a bright welcome.")[33] And even magnanimous Stamp, having run through a litany of white men's crimes—"whole towns wiped clean of Negroes; eighty-seven lynchings in one year alone in Kentucky; four colored schools burned to the ground; grown men whipped like children; children whipped like adults," and then finding something particularly horrible, a red ribbon "knotted around a curl of wet wooly hair, clinging still to its bit of scalp"—even Stamp Paid is compelled to ask himself, "What *are* these people? You tell me, Jesus. What *are* they?"[34]

The act of deliverance in the book comes when Sethe sets out and attacks a white man who reminds her, through her delusional haze, of the man who had come years ago to take her and her children back to slavery. This time, instead of attacking her own she attacks her victimizer, or his semblance. The semblance is nothing other than a white liberal, a man, old now, who in his youth had been active in the Ohio antislavery movement. It's then that Beloved, the preying ghost of the murdered child, finally disappears. The restoration of the town's black community begins from the day that Sethe fights back; and her potential happiness, such as it will be, also begins there.

It's healthier to attack than be attacked, better to marvel at the baseness of white people—What are they? Are they even human?—than to have your own humanity called into question by them. A ghost is a form of repetition, a form of guilt. By her attack, Sethe presumably shifts the burden of guilt, undoes repetition, gets rid of the ghost (if only for a while). For the black reader *Beloved* offers the vision of a community restored to solid trust after the horrible day when, out of envy, no one came to warn Sethe that the slave-catchers were on the way. It's the white community, authors of the Holocaust, that's now to be haunted. This book, a work of genius, seeks to effect a transference; from black to white, the guilt for slavery must go.

The Gothic burden isn't overcome so much as it is shifted—the crime of slavery finds its true culprit. But as to how to overcome guilt and shame and the sorry weight of the past through some action in the present, the book offers no conception. In Shelley's language, *Beloved* simply puts Jupiter where Prometheus was, the white race in the guilty state where the black race had been. Satisfying as that might be, at least to black readers, it leaves the domination of the Gothic intact. America, in this vision, remains haunted.

Beloved, stunning work that it is, reaffirms the division of the races. Perhaps it helps a little to make the world safe for other Gothic "novels," like the two versions of the O. J. Simpson case, the African American and the white Gothic. The latter, written in the imaginations of the American majority, is the tale of a depraved hero-villain named O. J. Simpson, whose evil demon finally took over. And that evil demon, as *Newsweek, Time,* and other sources always stopped just short of making completely clear, was his black self.

In the black-Gothic O. J. novel, society has become a Gothic institution, its evil concentrated in the machinations of the disturbed detective Mark Fuhrman and the Los Angeles Police Department. What we got from popular renderings of the O. J. Simpson case was more Gothic, more victims and villains, more cultural sadomasochism, and a deeper division of the races. For both Gothic novels, the white and the black, are instances of dead-end Gothic. That's how blacks are, goes one diagnosis; that's how the white system works, goes the other: then a mutual throwing up of hands.

What Morrison knows and brutally renders is that race vies and combines with sadomasochism for the position of Gothic topos par excellence in current-day America. For many, if not most, of the Gothic events I have described in this book have race as a major element: not just O. J. and Michael Jackson, but Susan Smith and the black man who supposedly took her children; not just Poe with his visions of Dirk Peters, but also Mailer with his White Negro and Kesey with Chief Broom. We come again and again to the old traumas and griefs. Perhaps the great visionary Gothic work of our century, our *Prometheus Unbound*, will be the one that unlocks racial hatred in the way that Shelley unlocks the subject of revenge and the sadomasochistic impulse. For that we would need an artist who could be as honest about his or her attractions to racism as Shelley, in a purported age of liberation, was willing to be about his attractions to absolutism and sadomasochism.

Whatever cultural antidotes to our Gothic fixations are likely to arise, I don't think that they are going to come from religion. American religion now is, with some exceptions, becoming progressively more intolerant and literal-minded in its designs. We live in a moment of fundamentalist upsurge. The emphasis on religious difference that worshipers now insist on too often boils down into a distinction between the damned and the saved, between darkness and self-important light. This way of mapping the world is redolent of Gothic in its more dismally reductive forms. The most fruitful response to Gothic lies not, I believe, in regression toward crude religious belief (regression toward longing for the father, longing for the mother), but in the further deployment of the human imagination, of the vision of life pitted against the strong and inexorable pressures of death.

But sadly enough, despite the example of Kushner and Morrison and a few others, our culture remains in many ways divided between Gothic and visionary impulses. And of the two, Gothic is surely ascendant. The fact that artists with the prowess of Morrison and Kushner can't, despite a hunger for redemption, transform the Gothic, is strong testimony to the force of the haunted vision.

Perhaps in time there will come along creators who can look hard-eyed at our worst Gothic fears and not retreat from them into fantasies of renewal like *Iron John* and *Forrest Gump*. Maybe they will take Gothic pessimism as a starting point and come up with visions that, while affirmative, never forget the authentic darkness that Gothic art discloses. I would like to go further in describing such works of art and intellectual imagination, but it is at this point that the critic is compelled to step aside and the artist to take over.

⊓⊙TES

PREFACE

1. *John Keats: The Collected Poems*, ed. John Barnard (New York: Penguin, 1979), p. 459.

2. Barbara Grizzuti Harrison, "The Importance of Being Oprah," *The New York Times Magazine*, June 11, 1989, p. 28.

AMERICAN GOTHIC

1. Chris Baldick, ed., *The Oxford Book of Gothic Tales* (Oxford: Oxford University Press, 1993), p. xix.

2. Eve Kosofsky Sedgwick, *The Coherence of Gothic Conventions* (New York: Arno Press, 1980), pp. 8–9.

3. Evan Thomas, "The Double Life of O. J. Simpson," *Newsweek*, August 29, 1994, pp. 43–49.

4. *Time*, June 27, 1994.

5. Jeffrey Toobin, *The Run of His Life: The People v. O. J. Simpson* (New York: Random House, 1996), p. 244.

6. "Nicole Simpson's Character Attacked," *Washington Post*, October 25, 1996, p. A3.

7. Leslie Fiedler, *Love and Death in the American Novel*, 3rd ed. (1960; rpt. New York: Anchor Books, 1992), p. 133.

8. Fiedler, *Love and Death*, p. 127.

9. Joyce Carol Oates, *Zombie* (New York: Dutton, 1995).

10. July 17, 1995, p. 29.

11. Carol Clover, *Men, Women, and Chain Saws: Gender in the Modern Horror Film* (Princeton: Princeton University Press, 1992), pp. 32–35.

12. Marquis de Sade, *The 120 Days of Sodom and Other Writings*, comp. and trans. Austryn Wainhouse and Richard Seaver (New York: Grove Press, 1966), p. 109.

13. Edmund Burke, *Reflections on the Revolution in France and on the Proceedings in Certain Societies in London Relative to that Event*, ed. Conor Cruise O'Brien (1790; rpt. New York: Penguin Books, 1981), p. 333.

14. Burke, *Reflections*, p. 164.

15. See Montague Summers, *The Gothic Quest: A History of the Gothic Novel* (1938; rpt. New York: Russell & Russell, 1964), p. 29.

16. Chris Baldick, *In Frankenstein's Shadow: Myth, Monstrosity, and Nineteenth-Century Writing* (Oxford: Clarendon Press, 1987), pp. 128–131.

17. Susan Sontag, *Against Interpretation* (New York: Anchor, 1966), pp. 209–225.

18. Bill McKibben, *The End of Nature* (New York: Random House, 1989).

19. Susan Sontag, "AIDS and Its Metaphors," *The New York Review of Books*, October 27, 1988, pp. 88–98 (quotation on p. 94).

20. Baldick, *Oxford Book of Gothic Tales*, p. xix.

21. Cited in *The New Republic*, March 18, 1996, p. 17.

22. Camille Paglia, *Vamps and Tramps: New Essays* (New York: Vintage, 1994), pp. 67–70.

23. Camille Paglia, *Sexual Personae: Art and Decadence from Nefertiti to Emily Dickinson* (New Haven: Yale University Press, 1990).

24. *Harper's Magazine*, August 1995, p. 13.

25. "What Are We Doing On-Line?" *Harper's Magazine* Forum, August 1995, p. 44 (John Perry Barlow is the speaker).

26. Marina Warner, *Six Myths of Our Time* (New York: Random House, 1994), pp. 43–62.

27. Richard Ofshe and Ethan Watters, *Making Monsters: False Memories, Psychotherapy, and Sexual Hysteria* (New York: Scribner's, 1994), p. 177.

28. Frederick Crews, "The Revenge of the Repressed," *New York Review of Books*, November 17, 1994, pp. 54–60 (the quotation is on p. 58).

29. Slavoj Žižek, *Looking Awry: An Introduction to Jacques Lacan through Popular Culture* (Cambridge, Mass.: MIT Press, 1991), p. 23.

30. *Foucault Reader,* ed. Paul Rabinow (New York: Pantheon, 1984), p. 61.

31. Thanks to Susan Fraiman for this point.

32. Ann Radcliffe, *The Mysteries of Udolpho* (1794; rpt. New York: Oxford University Press, 1991), p. 358.

33. Marilyn Butler, *Romantics, Rebels, and Reactionaries: English Literature and Its Background, 1760–1830* (Oxford: Oxford University Press, 1981), p. 95.

34. Matthew Gregory Lewis, *The Monk* (1796; rpt. New York: Grove Press, 1952), p. 420.

35. *Blake: Complete Writings,* ed. Geoffrey Keynes (London: Oxford University Press, 1966), p. 216.

36. Fiedler, *Love and Death,* p. 135.

37. Charles Baxter, "Dysfunctional Narratives or 'Mistakes Were Made,'" *Ploughshares,* Fall 1994, pp. 67–82 (quotation is on pp. 72–73).

38. Paul Wilkes, "Unholy Acts," *The New Yorker,* June 7, 1993; pp. 62–79 (quotation is on p. 71).

39. Wilkes, "Unholy Acts," p. 79.

40. Toobin, *The Run of His Life,* p. 11.

41. Fiedler, *Love and Death,* p. 129.

The World according to Forrest Gump

1. Harold Bloom, *Poetics of Influence* (New Haven: Schwab, 1988), pp. 284, 285.

2. Newt Gingrich, *To Renew America* (New York: Harper Collins, 1995), p. 55.

3. December 27, 1993, pp. 56–65.

4. Harold Bloom, *Omens of Millennium: The Gnosis of Angels, Dreams, and Resurrection* (New York: Riverhead Books, 1996), p. 44.

5. Camille Paglia, *Sexual Personae: Art and Decadence from Nefertiti to Emily Dickinson* (New Haven: Yale University Press, 1990), p. 521.

6. Mark Crispin Miller, "The Great Driving Power of Our System," *Adbusters,* Winter 1995, pp. 7–12 (the quotations are on p. 8 and p. 11).

7. Naomi Wolf, *The Beauty Myth: How Images of Beauty Are Used against Women* (New York: Doubleday, 1991), p. 134.

8. Wolf, *Beauty Myth,* p. 134,

9. Laura Mulvey, "Visual Pleasure and Narrative Cinema," in *Feminisms: An Anthology of Literary Theory and Criticism,* ed. Robyn R. Warhol

and Diane Price Herndl (New Brunswick: Rutgers University Press, 1991), pp. 432–442.

10. Robert Bly, *Iron John: A Book about Men* (New York: Random House, 1990), p. 6.

11. Andrew Ross, "Wet, Dark, and Low, Eco-Man Evolves from Eco-Woman," *Boundary 2*, 19:2 (Spring 1992), pp. 205–232.

12. Bly, *Iron John*, p. 143.

13. *The Poetry of Robert Frost*, ed. Edward Connery Lathem (New York: Holt, Rinehart and Winston, 1967), p. 208.

14. Clarissa Pinkola Estés, *Women Who Run with the Wolves: Myths and Stories of the Wild Woman Archetype* (New York: Ballantine, 1995).

15. John Bradshaw, *Home Coming: Reclaiming and Championing Your Inner Child* (New York: Bantam, 1992), p. 92.

16. David Rieff, "Victims, All?" *Harper's Magazine*, October 1991, pp. 49–56.

17. Allen Ginsberg, *Howl* (San Francisco: City Lights Books, 1976), p. 9.

18. William Wordsworth, *The Prelude*, ed. Jonathan Wordsworth (New York: Viking, 1995), p. 441.

19. Jane Austen, *Northanger Abbey*, ed. John Davie (New York: Oxford University Press, 1990), p. 25.

20. Austen, *Northanger Abbey*, p. 110.

21. Katherine Spurlock, *Rival Authorities: Sigmund Freud, T. S. Eliot, and the Interpretation of Culture* (Ph.D. diss., University of Virginia, 1997).

22. Clement Greenberg, *The Collected Essays and Criticism*, ed. John O'Brian, 4 vols. (Chicago: University of Chicago Press, 1986), 2: 322–326 (the quotation is on p. 323).

23. Greenberg, *Collected Essays and Criticism*, 2: 326.

24. Austen, *Northanger Abbey*, p. 128.

25. Anthony Vidler, *The Architectural Uncanny: Essays in the Modern Unhomely* (Cambridge: MIT Press, 1992), p. 64.

26. Le Corbusier, *Towards a New Architecture*, trans. Frederick Etchells (New York: Payson & Clarke, 1923), p. 227.

27. Gaston Bachelard, *The Poetics of Space*, trans. Maria Jolas (Boston: Beacon Press, 1964), p. 6.

S & M Culture

1. J. H. van den Berg, *The Changing Nature of Man: Introduction to a Historical Psychology*, trans. H. F. Croes (New York: Delta, 1961), p. 232.

2. *The Standard Edition of the Complete Psychological Works of Sigmund Freud*, trans. James Strachey et al., 24 vols. (London: Hogarth Press, 1953) (hereafter *"S.E."*), 21: 129.

3. Michel Foucault, *Madness and Civilization: A History of Insanity in the Age of Reason*, trans. Richard Howard (London: Tavistock Press, 1965), p. 97

4. Melinda Blau, "Ordinary People," *New York Magazine*, November 28, 1994, pp. 39–46.

5. Leo Bersani, *Homos* (Cambridge: Harvard University Press, 1995), pp. 83–89.

6. Friedrich Nietzsche, *Thus Spoke Zarathustra*, trans. Walter Kaufmann (New York: Penguin, 1966), p. 140.

7. *Shelley: Poetical Works*, ed. Thomas Hutchinson (London: Oxford University Press, 1967), p. 238.

8. *S.E.* 21: 90, n.1.

9. *The Portable Coleridge*, ed. I. A. Richards (New York: Viking, 1984), p. 90.

10. *Shelley*, p. 208.

11. *Poe: Poetry and Tales*, ed. Patrick F. Quinn (New York: Library of America, 1984), p. 555.

12. *Shelley*, p. 214.

13. *Poe*, p. 829.

14. Martin Heidegger, *Nietzsche, Volume 2: The Eternal Recurrence of the Same*, trans. David Farrell Krell (San Francisco: Harper & Row, 1984) p. 20.

15. Friedrich Nietzsche, *The Gay Science*, trans. Walter Kaufmann (New York: Vintage, 1974), p. 273.

16. Leslie Fiedler, *Love and Death in the American Novel*, 3rd ed. (1960; rpt. New York: Anchor Books, 1992), pp. 33–34.

17. Harold Bloom, *The Anxiety of Influence: A Theory of Poetry* (New York: Oxford, 1973), p. 39.

18. Friedrich Nietzsche, *The Birth of Tragedy and the Genealogy of Morals*, trans. Frances Golffing (New York: Doubleday, 1956), p. 93.

19. Nietzsche, *Birth of Tragedy*, p. 93.

20. Arnold Hauser, *The Social History of Art*, trans. Stanley Godman, 4 vols. (New York: Random House, 1951), 3: 212–213.

21. Northrop Frye, *Fables of Identity: Studies in Poetic Mythology* (New York: Harcourt, Brace & World, 1963), p. 177.

22. Frye, *Fables of Identity*, p. 176.

NOTES TO PAGES 127-167

23. Camille Paglia, *Sexual Personae: Art and Decadence from Nefertiti to Emily Dickinson* (New Haven: Yale University Press, 1990), p. 359.

24. Ross Posnock, "Roy Cohn in America," *Raritan* 13:3 (Winter 1994), p. 71.

25. Tony Kushner, *Angels in America: A Gay Fantasia on National Themes; Part One: Millennium Approaches* (New York: Theatre Communications Group, 1993), p. 11.

26. Kushner, *Millennium Approaches*, p. 45.

27. Tony Kushner, *Angels in America, Part Two: Perestroika* (New York: Theatre Communications Group, 1994), p. 95.

28. Kushner, *Perestroika*, p. 30.

29. Kushner, *Perestroika*, pp. 76, 78.

30. Kushner, *Perestroika*, pp. 77–78.

31. Kushner, *Perestroika*, p. 148.

32. Stanley Crouch, *Notes of a Hanging Judge: Essays and Reviews, 1979–1989* (New York: Oxford University Press, 1990), p. 205.

33. Toni Morrison, *Beloved* (New York: Knopf, 1987), pp. 171, 172.

34. Morrison, *Beloved*, p. 180.

INDEX